THE ITALIANS

HOW THEY LIVE AND WORK

Volumes in the series

THE ARGENTINES, by Dereck Foster

THE DUTCH, by Ann Hoffman

THE FRENCH, by Joseph T. Carroll

THE GREEKS, by T.R.B. Dicks

THE IRISH, by Martin Wallace

THE ITALIANS, by Andrew Bryant

THE SPANIARDS, by Michael Perceval

THE SWEDES, by Paul Britten Austin

THE WEST GERMANS, by Reginald Peck

THE ITALIANS
How They Live and Work

Andrew Bryant

Revised Edition

PRAEGER PUBLISHERS
New York · Washington

BOOKS THAT MATTER

Published in the United States of America in 1969
Revised edition 1971
by Praeger Publishers, Inc
111 Fourth Avenue, New York, N.Y. 10003

© 1968, 1971, in England by Andrew Bryant

Second printing 1973

Library of Congress Catalog Number: 76-150698

Printed in Great Britain

Contents

INTRODUCTION   11

I   THE COUNTRY AND THE PEOPLE   13
Chief physical characteristics . upper or continental
Italy . climate . racial derivation . population .
language . national characteristics . historical land-
marks . the Renascence . the Risorgimento

II   HOW THE COUNTRY IS RUN   37
Regions and cities . local government . ministries .
political parties . religion . currency . taxation .
the army . the navy . the air force . legal and penal
systems . the legal profession . criminal jurisdiction . police

III   HOW THEY LIVE   67
Housing . modern conveniences . servants . what
they eat and drink . how they spend their money .
medical services . hospitals . social security

IV   HOW THEY WORK   84
Electricity . nuclear energy . petroleum . methane . marble . mineral resources . iron and
steel . engineering industries . shipbuilding . motor
vehicles . aircraft . other heavy engineering . light
engineering . electronics . the chemical industry .
rubber . textiles . cotton . artificial fibres . wool .
artisans and craftsmen . finance . agriculture .
agrarian reform and land reclamation . agricultural
produce . fisheries . forests . the Southern Development Fund . shops . foreign trade . trade fairs .
seaports and shipping . trade unions and employers'
organisations . unemployment . women at work .
sickness and injury benefits . poor relief

V   HOW THEY LEARN   130
Schools . universities . academies and institutes .
grants

VI   HOW THEY GET ABOUT   137
Railways . roads . air traffic . waterways . Straits
of Messina

VII   HOW THEY AMUSE THEMSELVES   148
The theatre . opera . music . the cinema . radio
and television . newspapers . libraries and publishing . sport and recreation . Dopolavoro . holidays

VIII   HINTS FOR VISITORS   158

INDEX   161

List of Illustrations

	Page
The Highway of the Sun finds its way across the Apennines	17
Calabrian peasant women	18
A typical southern scene	35
The workers' canteen in a petrochemical factory in Brindisi	36
The Grand Canal at Venice	53
Treating olive trees at Prima Porta	54
A modern quarter at Rome	71
The Quirinal Palace at Rome	71
A view in the Piazza della Signoria at Florence	72
View of the nuclear centre at Frascati	89
An aircraft factory at Turin	89
Fishermen at Naples hauling a catch on to Via Caracciolo	90
In the ricefields of Piedmont	90
Ceramic workers at Chianciano, near Siena in Tuscany	90
Elementary school at Coroglio in the province of Como	107
The University of Parma	108
A retractable gangway at Fiumicino airport near Rome	125
Villagers playing bowls	126
Football and sports stadiums	143
A football match with medieval rules at Florence	144
The 'Bridge Game', a contest, recalling a battle of 1509	144

Acknowledgments:
I wish to express my thanks to Rag. Chillemi
of the Information Office, Rome, for the
information and photographs very cour-
teously supplied. Acknowledgments are also
due to the Casa Fotografica Vaghi of Parma
for the photograph of the university of
Parma on page 108, and to Sig. Erminio
Lenza of the Grotte di Pompeo restaurant,
Campo de' Fiori, Rome, for the menu
quoted on page 77.

Sources:
Information obtained from publications of
The Central Institute of Statistics, Rome,
and other publications.
The Economic Background: Lutz, V. Italy:
An Economic Study. O.U.P., 1962.
Walker, D. S.: A Geography of Italy.
Methuen, 1958.

New Post Office address basic code numbers in force from 1 July 1967

ITALY BEFORE UNIFICATION 1847

1 Savoy: ceded to France in 1860	9 Duchy of Lucca (to Tuscany)
	9a Massa-Carrara
2 Piedmont	10 Grand Duchy of Tuscany
3 Sardinia	11 Papal States (enclave San Marino)
4 Nice: ceded to France in 1860	
5 South Tyrol (annexed 1919)	12 Kingdom of the Two Sicilies
6 (L) Lombardy—Veneto (V)	13 Istria (incorporated 1919-1945)
7 Duchy of Parma	14 Corsica (to France 1768)
8 Duchy of Modena	15 Malta

From Shepherd's Historical Atlas. No. 161

These divisions may be compared with the boundaries of the modern regions

Introduction

WHEN we think of Italy, or of most other countries, we have in mind a moral and spiritual reality, not only a physical and political one. The bounds of the country are well defined, yet it was never a separate political unity, not even in ancient times, until 1870. And the unity imposed from the north cannot be said even now to have gained profound hold upon the consciousness of the people. But Italy has always been a single cultural reality, unmistakable, powerful, and brilliant. The *magna mater virum*—the great mother of men—of Virgil, the oldest country in the West, the most deeply civilised, the teacher of Europe, the site and origin of a dozen great cultural periods, of a great universal State and a great universal vision, has never ceased to devote her spiritual riches to the rest of the world. The greatest European minds have acknowledged the dominating and decisive effect upon their lives of their experience of Italy.

Today the land and the people are being transformed in a still further outburst of energy and verve, creativity and inventiveness, adopting the gains of the Industrial Revolution—so far largely belonging to other countries—and adapting them to their own cultural forms. Until the time of the French Revolution the rest of Europe generally received from the peninsula much more than it contributed to it. Then the tide turned. Waves of liberalism, industrialism, nationalism, developed capitalism, socialism, mechanisation, communism, and much else, broke over the crystallised forms of the ancient life. Fascism has been described as the last stand of traditional Italy against the new forces that were so powerfully pervading her. Fascism collapsed and the country barely escaped obliteration by the Anglo-Americans. Italians learnt much from that experience and reprieve. Since she has become part of the United States' sphere of influence, Italy has taken advantage of the opportunities offered by American capital and skill, and is consequently adopting a new way of living. She is doing so with a brio and a degree of awareness that show that she is in no lasting danger of losing her own human riches and mighty cultural achievement, reflected in the instinctive wisdom with which the ever-changing real world is being dealt with. So rapid, deep and dynamic are the changes going on that a book like this, setting out to describe the process, risks being outrun by events. Therefore emphasis has been placed on what is about to be done, rather than on what has been done or is even being done, for the Italian future is swiftly becoming the present.

I

The Country and the People

CHIEF PHYSICAL CHARACTERISTICS

THREE great peninsulas extend from the southern coasts of Europe into the Mediterranean Sea. The Italian Republic consists largely of the middle, boot-shaped one, and its adjacent islands and a large arc of territory extending into the mainland of Europe. It lies in the temperate zone, and is about 730 miles long and has an average width of 130 miles. By comparison, Great Britain lies in the northern part of the temperate zone, but looks towards the Arctic Circle, whereas Italy points towards the Equator; England and Scotland together are 608 miles long, and England is 320 miles wide at its greatest breadth; like Italy, Britain is a kind of appendix to Europe, pointing away towards other continents, but, whereas the sea has cut Britain off from many influences, it has always exposed Italy to them. The Italian Republic includes the big islands of Sicily and Sardinia; the former is separated from the peninsula only by the very narrow straits of Messina, but Sardinia lies about 150 miles to the west. The islands of Corsica and Malta pertain to Italy geographically and culturally, but not politically; Corsica has been a Department of France since 1796, and Malta is an independent state.

Italy is bounded in the north by the great semicircular range of the Alps, which runs uninterruptedly from the sea at Ventimiglia on the French frontier in the north-west, around by

Switzerland and Austria to Yugoslavia on the north-east. Its coasts extend for 5,300 miles and are washed by the Ligurian Sea (north-west), the Tyrrhenian Sea (west), the Ionian Sea (south) and the Adriatic Sea (east). The peninsula forms a bridge, together with Sicily, across the Mediterranean and is the natural link with Africa and the Near East for central and central-southern Europe. The whole area of the Republic, with the numerous small islands, amounts to 116,280 square miles. The area of Great Britain is 89,038 square miles and 94,500 with Northern Ireland. The territories of Italy enclose two small independent states: the Vatican City (108.7 acres and various enclaves) and the Republic of San Marino (23.8 square miles).

There is a primary distinction between continental or Upper Italy and peninsular and insular Italy. Upper Italy consists of the great alluvial plain of the valley of the river Po and the surrounding Alps. The southern border of this region is the Apennine range, which corresponds obliquely with the line where the peninsular part of the country begins, extending from the Mediterranean Sea at Genoa to above Rimini on the Adriatic. The chief alpine regions are the Gran Paradiso in the north-west and the Dolomites in the north. Some of the highest peaks in Europe lie along these ranges: Monte Rosa (15,217 ft), the Matterhorn (14,780 ft), but it should be remembered that the Alps have never been a barrier between Italy and the rest of Europe, however formidable they may seem; all history shows this, and one has only to see how low and easy to cross is such a pass as the Brenner to understand it. The main passes are the Little St Bernard, to France, the Great St Bernard, to France (where there is now a road tunnel), the Simplon, to Switzerland, the Brenner, between South Tyrol and North Tyrol, and the Tarvisio Pass into Carinthia in Austria.

UPPER OR CONTINENTAL ITALY

Its vast alluvial flats, its endless supplies of water, its great irrigation works, the richness of the soil, the warmth of the climate and the industry of the population have made the valley of the Po one of the greatest agricultural and cultural areas of Europe. It has an area of 16,000 square miles and contains three-fifths of all level land to be found in Italy. Some of the land near the mouths of the Po lies below the level of the sea. The Po descends from the Maritime or Western Alps and flows eastwards for 405 miles, collecting water from many streams coming down from both the Alps and the Apennines, to north and south of it; it crosses the Plain of Lombardy and the Veneto and enters the sea south of Venice. Its chief left-hand tributaries are the Ticino, the Adda and the Mincio, which flow out of Lake Maggiore, Lake Como and Lake Garda respectively, and the Oglio which flows from Lake Iseo. Its chief right-hand tributaries (from the Apennines) are the Tanaro, Trebbia, Tavo and Secchia. The other chief rivers of Upper Italy are the Adige, which begins as the Etsch in the Middle Alps and flows parallel to and north of the Po, and the Piave, Brenta and Tagliamento, which flow from the Dolomites and the Eastern Alps to the sea above Venice.

The Western or Maritime Alps reach the sea at Ventimiglia, and then run along the coast eastwards and southwards as the Ligurian Alps; they meet the Apennines, which continue the relief south-eastward, and then southward and westward again to the Straits of Messina and into Sicily, forming as it were the backbone of Italy and the chief characteristic of the peninsular region.

The peninsula begins at the line already indicated as the southern limit of the North Italian plain. From the Genoa-Rimini line southwards the Apennines consist of the Ligurian, Etruscan and Roman, Abruzzi, Apulian, Sila and Aspromonte ranges (the last two in the toe of Italy). The chain is rugged, but generally not very high, except in the Abruzzi and the Sila and Aspromonte ' rugged mountain ' sections (Gran Sasso d'Italia in the Abruzzi, 9,560 ft; Mt Corno, 7,537 ft). The western sides of the ranges, especially around Rome and Naples, show clear signs of recent volcanic activity, and several offshore island mountains, such as Stromboli, are still active. The most remarkable volcanoes are Vesuvius on the mainland and Etna in Sicily.

The land on the western side of the ranges was under sea until fairly recent times, and the whole line is still unsettled, as continuing earthquakes and eruptions indicate. There are many lakes of volcanic origin (Lake Trasimene, Lake Bracciano, Lake of Nemi etc).

The dominating mountain ranges are one of the reasons for the exceptional, magical, beauty of Italy. They also show that the peninsula is geologically young in comparison with northern Europe. The Po valley and the western littoral were slow to rise and be silted up from the sea between the mountains. The eastern littoral is narrow (average width 30 miles), and descends more steeply.

The rivers on both the western and eastern slopes are shorter and have more irregular courses than those of Upper Italy. Especially in the south, they have a torrential course, and many of the smaller ones flow fully only at long intervals, not unlike African wadis. The chief peninsular rivers are the Arno (149 miles), and the Tiber (157 miles), both on the western littoral and mainly notable for the famous cities that stand on their banks; others, in the vicinity of Naples, are the Volturno, the Garigliano and the Sele. All the rivers of Italy are subject to flooding; the Po overruns it banks frequently, especially in places where it

———

The Highway of the Sun finds its way across the Apennines between Bologna and Florence, through the passes where the consul Flaminius built the Flaminian Way 2,200 years ago.

normally flows above the level of the surrounding countryside. The Arno flooded Florence catastrophically in November 1966. The main river of Sicily is the Simeto, which flows through the plain of Enna near Catania; the Tirso is the most notable river in Sardinia.

CLIMATE

Italy has a wide range of climates, because of its extension through several latitudes and because of its situation and the diversity of its mountains and plains. The principal factor in making the climate is the Mediterranean Sea, which is warm in the winter-time. The southern prospect, facing Africa, is the next most important element. Winters are generally short and mild, except in the Alps; summers are long and tranquil, with uniform temperatures; spring and autumn are long and gradual, and autumn is notably warmer than spring. This last is a characteristic mark of a maritime climate. The alpine regions have much rain and snow, low winter temperatures and many temperature variations throughout the year, but because they face the south their weather is appreciably milder than that of the northern slopes of the Alps; a difference of as much as 10°C

Old Italy is very much alive, as the vigour of these Calabrian peasant women shows.

B

is noticeable in the summer between north and south of the Alps. The mildest climate in the peninsula is probably that of the Ligurian riviera, below Genoa, which is warmed by its position in the winter and cooled by sea breezes in the summer.

Most rain falls in the autumn and spring, but some falls in every month, and prolonged droughts are not common, except perhaps in Sicily. Rain falls on about 100 days a year, and averages vary from 20 to 80 inches a year. The rainiest parts are naturally the heights, particularly those which are near the sea. Snow sometimes falls even in places such as Rome and Naples; it is more common in northern cities such as Milan and Turin, but only on the ranges does it remain for any great length of time. Summers are very hot in Sicily and southern Italy, but winters are very mild.

The prevailing climatic conditions are tempered by four great winds—the Maestrale (Mistral), the Bora, the Tramontana, and the Scirocco. The Maestrale descends from the valley of the Rhône and central Europe upon Liguria and Genoa in the winter; it is very strong and bitterly cold, and can cause danger to shipping, even in ports. The Bora (the word means ' wind ' in Serbo-Croat) descends upon Trieste and the Adriatic from Siberia; ropes and handrails have to be supplied for pedestrians in Trieste when it is blowing. The Tramontana is a cold north-north-easterly which blows in clear skies from snowfields over central Italy in the winter and early spring, and is also bitterly cold; it is well known in Rome. The Scirocco, finally, blows from the Sahara; it is hot and dry when it begins in Africa, but collects moisture over the sea and blows upon the Tyrrhenian and Sicilian coasts as a humid, stifling wind. It usually marks the onset of summer in Rome.

RACIAL DERIVATION

There is no such thing as a Latin race today; there is of course a Latin culture to which populations of many racial origins belong. The present population of Italy is descended from many groups, tribes, peoples and nations which have settled in the peninsula over the last three thousand years. The Latin strain, in other words the face and head of Julius Caesar, may still be seen in many places, especially in the remoter parts of the mountains near Rome. The Mediterranean type may prevail, yet there are innumerable varieties, groups of which often occur within quite short distances of each other : descendants of ancient Greeks and Etruscans, of the original Italic inhabitants who preceded those settlers, of the people who became the Romans proper, Syrians, Africans, Iberians and many other strains brought in over the centuries; Sicily was once an Arab kingdom, and the Semitic type of features is still noticeable there. The Normans who succeeded the Arabs there and in southern Italy left clear traces of themselves (one of the oldest Norman families in Italy, the Rufo family, is collaterally descended from William Rufus, king of England). The territory between the Alps and the Apennines was settled by Celts for centuries before the Romans colonised and latinised the inhabitants (who thereupon produced Catullus, Virgil and Livy). The peasantry of the Veneto near the Yugoslav border has strong Slav strains in it; the Gothic, Lombard and other Germanic conquerors of the period following the fall of the Roman Empire, though relatively few, left distinct traces of themselves, especially in the population of Lombardy and Piedmont. Today there are Albanian and Greek areas in Apulia and Sicily; the regions of Venezia-Giulia and Friuli both have very large Slav populations, and there is a whole German province—South Tyrol—within the frontiers of the Republic. But the blond Germanic type represents only about two per cent of the whole population, and the general complexion, at least in the eyes of a foreigner, is dark. The Mediterranean type, with abundant black hair, olive skin and dark eyes certainly prevails over all other types, yet the population is really as varied as the population of a country like Britain. The average height is about 5 ft 6 in, and is increasing. There are many Gipsies.

POPULATION

On 1 January 1967 the population numbered 53,350,200 (population of the United Kingdom 52,708,934 in 1961). The increase in population since 1965 has amounted to about four million, and this increase is about equal to the growth in the population of Great Britain in the same period. The working class accounts for 56.8 per cent of the population. The most salient difference in population distribution between Great Britain and Italy is that whereas the vast majority of the British live in cities and large towns, Italians are much more evenly distributed between town and country. About half reside in communes (municipalities) with populations of less than 20,000, 22.8 per cent of the total population live in towns and villages of less than 5,000 inhabitants, and only 15.1 per cent in cities with more than 500,000 inhabitants. As in Great Britain, about half the population works (20,000,000 in 1961-5), but in different proportions as regards industries than in Great Britain. In 1961-5 27.5 per cent of the Italian working population was employed in agriculture, 39 per cent in industry and 33 per cent in professions, trades and services. This contrasts with the situation in Britain, where only about 2.2 per cent of the population is engaged in agriculture and the rest work in various kinds of industry. The phenomenon of concentration of population around great industrial centres, so marked in Britain, where 30 million of the whole population live in the region 65 miles wide and 200 miles long, extending from the Thames to the Mersey, is now taking shape in Italy. The northern region, or Upper Italy, had a population of 23,853,000 in 1966, because of its great concentrations of industries; the central region had only 9,888,000 inhabitants, and the south 19,189,000. The south has the highest birth rate and the lowest death rate in the whole country. Yet the population of the northern region increased by 10 per cent in 1956-66 while that of the south increased by only 4 per cent. This shows that the population is moving out of the south into the northern industrial regions.

There is a general movement away from the countryside into the bigger towns and cities. The average density of population is about 450 per square mile, whereas the figure for Britain is 863 per square mile. The death rate of about 11 per cent a year is a little higher than that of Britain (about 10 per cent); the birth rate is higher, and there is a natural increase of about 9.5 per cent a year (5.3 per cent in Britain). But both birth and death rates are falling, and so is the marriage rate. In 1964 it was already lower than the rate in Britain in 1965 (Italy, 1964, 417,486; Britain, 1965, 421,700 or 15.6 per cent). In 1966 there were only 385,046 marriages in Italy.

There are forty cities with populations of over 100,000, and their presence must be taken into account when considering regional population densities. Latium (Lazio) has a high density because it contains Rome (nearly 3 million inhabitants). The most densely-populated regions are in fact the Campania (of which Naples is the capital), Liguria (Genoa) and Latium. Friuli-Venezia Giulia in the far north-east and Tuscany occupy a middle position; the most thinly-populated parts are the Val d'Aosta, Sardinia and Basilicata (between the heel and toe of the peninsula). As we shall see later, the population of Italy is socially organised on a strongly regional basis. Although deeply attached to their soil and their native villages, the Italians have at all times shown a genius for creating urban life and beautiful cities. It is a curious fact that in the language the word for town *(paese)* is the same as the word for Country *(Paese)*. The word for countryside is *campagna*. Especially in the south, the agricultural population lives in walled hilltop towns and goes out to its fields every day. In the Middle Ages each big town won a territory for itself, and the intimate relations then established between each town and its countryside still exist. A man will not even think of himself as a Lombard, but as a Milanese, even though he comes from a village at some distance from Milan but still in its sphere of influence. Besides the big regional capitals, there are large numbers of smaller ancient cities, formerly of political and cultural importance and now still very much alive as local centres and remarkable for the art and architecture of their golden ages. Examples are Cremona, Mantua, Orvieto, Pisa, Urbino, Cortona, and Spoleto. There are many more.

LANGUAGE

The official language of the country is Italian, which is one of the Romance or Romanic languages, directly descended from Latin. It is used on all public occasions, on radio and television, for literature and in newspapers, and is taught to foreigners. It is usually regarded as being closer to Latin than any of the other Romanic languages. It must be described as a literary creation, owing its existence chiefly to the ideas and labours of Dante Alighieri in the fourteenth century and Alessandro Manzoni in the nineteenth. But Italy is the proud possessor of hundreds of dialects, which are spoken everywhere in preference to the official language and by all classes from the highest to the lowest. A number of these dialects have literatures of their own. The Italian language was formed by writers on the basis of the educated language of Tuscany, and the best form of speech is said to be *La lingua toscana in bocca romana*—The Tuscan tongue in the Roman mouth. Its vocabulary is highly Latin and the grammar is also clearly derived from Latin grammar. It is very musical, since vowels predominate over consonants, and it is capable of expressing many subtleties of thought and feeling in a delicate and sweet manner. Much of its peculiar expressiveness comes from its richness of diminutives, majoritives and other endings. It is capable of being as precise as any other language, yet it must be admitted that its faults are verbosity and cloudiness. But to see of what conciseness it is capable one has only to compare the Italian word *chiederglielo* and its English equivalent, for which no less than five words are needed: *to ask him for it*!

There are relatively very few foreign loan words, unlike in English, and yet English is almost as fully a Latin language as Italian. This does not mean that no one ever took any words from the foreigners who occupied Italy for so many centuries, but only that foreign words tend to be left in the dialects. The dialects of upper Italy contain numerous German words; Spanish, French and German words are also frequent in Neapolitan. Piedmontese is strongly affected by French, and Spanish, French and Arabic have a large part in the dialects of Sicily. Apart from such dialects, French is spoken widely in the Val d'Aosta; the population of South Tyrol speaks German; about half a million people in Friuli-Venezia Giulia speak Slovene and other Slav tongues, and Slav dialects are also found in the Molise region to the south of Rome. Ladin, a direct descendant from Latin, related to the Romanche language of Switzerland, is spoken in some valleys of the Dolomites; Greek and Albanian are spoken in Apulia and Sicily. Sardinia has its own language, and Catalan is spoken at Alghero in Sardinia. So numerous are the dialects that they are often mutually incomprehensible from one village to another. Italian therefore is useful in helping people from various parts to understand each other, and its influence is spreading through radio, television, military service and other means. It should be emphasised that in Italy class distinctions in speech are far less noticeable and far less important than they are with most people in England. They exist, but feelings of inferiority and superiority are not centred upon them.

NATIONAL CHARACTERISTICS

' People ask why Italians are not so popular outside of Italy. Perhaps the reason is the shock they experience when they find themselves away from this beautiful and good country, which is so elegant and wise . . . perhaps also because emigrants have already suffered much before they had to leave . . . But you Italians are so wise and tolerant, so mature and at the same time so vital, that you must try to understand that there is no one better than you! I am an Australian, and I have been living in Italy for eight years, and I am nostalgic for the smell of eucalyptus which comes to Sydney on the winds from the west. But living with you I have gained something that repays me for everything I have lost: your tolerance, your lack of narrowness of mind and fanaticism, all of which are very common in other countries. Finally, the best thing about you is your conviction that everything outside Italy is better, and this is the most fascinating thing of all about you; you are so humble . . .'

This is from a letter which a Mrs Lynette Dempsey Garibaldi wrote to the weekly magazine *Epoca* in January 1967, and it well expresses the feelings of admiration and delight which contact with Italy and its people rouses in the hearts of the vast majority of visitors. Many books could be written, and indeed have been written, about national characteristics, but on reading them one usually comes to feel that they are basically merely descriptions of all mankind. Nowhere is this impression greater than in the effort to seize the essence of the Italian character, the mystery of its charm, and the causes of its faults. What particular, divinely-inspired mingling of human and environmental elements produced this type out of the crucible of mankind? What are the general characteristics, and how shall we enumerate them?

Some of his qualities the Italian shares with other Mediterranean peoples; some again are his own. Just as tropical and northern plants transferred to the northern shores of the Mediterranean acquire a regularity of outline and a gloss and softness that was not theirs before, so man gains that sense of ease amongst the elements, trust in nature and an appearance of physical and inner completeness which first strikes the stranger in Italy. The fact that one knows that the sun will shine relatively mildly and constantly for at least ten months of the year, and that one can live without having to worry about whether it will be visible from day to day, as one does in the north, is the main factor in producing that basic belief in the kindness of creation which enables Mediterranean man to give freer play to his feelings and emotions and his nature generally than is possible for the northerner. The other factor, intimately bound up with that fundamental one, is the presence of a deep, ancient, comprehensive and unbroken cultural tradition, in which and upon which the Italian lives, whether he knows it or not.

He has a strong awareness of his own individual existence—the word *io*, I, is surely the most frequently uttered in the whole language—but he has an equally strong sense of belonging to a society, a chain of life, to which he always refers and by which his narcissism and individualism are tempered. In other words he is profoundly aware of belonging to a family, and no aspect of Italian life is comprehensible if the family, in which every individual is embedded, is left out of account. Young Italians do not look forward to marriage as a way of superior satisfactions alone, but as founding a family and finding happiness in devotion to their children. There is no word for home in the English sense; where a particular family may happen to live is not felt to be of great importance, but its influence is all-pervasive. The Italian's prime, often his only, loyalty is to it. There is little sense of that loyalty to organisations in which the British have excelled.

It is very difficult to speak of national characteristics. Regional and local characteristics are more important. Though there is little sharp class-consciousness, class differences do exist and are recognisable; the outlines are different from those in British society, and movement is far more fluid. The north and the south feel as much apart as do England and Scotland, or England and Ireland. The Venetian is quite different from the Roman. The Piedmontese type is dignified, distinguished, reserved, showing French influence; the Milanese is commercial, perhaps less refined, less sensitive; the Lombard is something different again. The Sicilian is easily distinguished by mainland Italians, though foreigners may not see the point of this distinction.

The ideals of behaviour to which Italians as a whole aspire are first and above all the moral and spiritual ideals of the Catholic Church, the influence of which, whether acknowledged or not, is radical, omnipresent and enormous, and secondly the social ideals of fraternity, which they practise easily; solitude, keeping oneself to oneself, privacy, have little or no value for them; affection is easily felt and easily expressed; aggressive feelings and behaviour are greatly deprecated and kept well out of the way.

They break through sometimes, and then a sudden, violent crime may occur. The Italian as a whole also feels a strong need to make a good show—*far bella figura*—and to be elegant; the Anglo-Saxon contraries of casualness and shabbiness are not only disliked but regarded as definitely insulting, since one owes it to one's company to dress 'decently so as to honour them no less than oneself. The immediate aim of social life for an Italian is to help establish an atmosphere of fraternity and spiritual well-being, in which everyone may share, and in which everyone aims not to exclude but to include as many as possible. Italians spend by far the greater part of their days engaged in this creative activity.

There is so far no mass of disorientated young people in Italy. There is some divergence between the ideal of womanhood and the treatment which women receive from their men, but there are varying situations in this regard from class to class. It has been said that Italian women are wonderful, and that their cross is Italian men. Yet Italy is the land of the cult of the Madonna and no country in Europe is so pregnant with female influences and characteristics. The reason may be that as a rule Italian women do not compete with men and so are able to exercise their own true qualities.

The Italian faults are a certain frivolity, proneness to generalisation, idealisation, and rationalisation which fail to take cognisance of the real situation, and devotion to words and sounds for their own sake. The most prominent virtues are devotion to family and children, to regions and cities, lack of agression, affability, genuine interest in other people, especially foreigners, sensitivity to art and beauty, creativity and inventiveness, a sense of tones, form, colour, light and air; in a word, a sunny, outward attitude to life.

HISTORICAL LANDMARKS

Italy may well be described as having been, from the viewpoint of the Eastern nations and of Greece, the America of the ancient world. It was inhabited only by stone-age peoples (the

Italics), of whom very little is known, until the Etruscans, Phoenicians and Greeks approached its shores in the first millenium before Christ. The Phoenicians colonised Sicily, Sardinia and Corsica. The Greeks settled in Sicily and all lower Italy, which came to be known as *Magna Graecia*—Greater Greece—much as lands in America were known as New France, New Spain, and New England. The Etruscans settled in the central part of the peninsula, probably coming from Asia Minor. The founders of the Roman line came in the same way. Recent archaeological finds have confirmed the old legends, upon which it used to be fashionable to cast so many doubts. Greek culture and civilisation were adopted and adapted by the Etruscans and the Romans, and Greece may still be perceived behind most things in Italy, especially in the south and particularly at Naples. By about the middle of the first millenium BC there were at least four distinct countries in the peninsula, in which the outlines of the present great regional divisions may already be seen : Celts in the north as far south as Bologna; Etruscans in the centre as far south as Rome; hill tribes and city states down the interior, and the Greek world of the south and Sicily. Rome gradually spread her command—her *imperium*—over all others, and so came into conflict with the outposts of the Carthaginian-Phoenician empire in Sicily, Sardinia and Corsica. Rome defeated Carthage in a hundred years' war ending in 146 BC. One result of this war was that Rome was obliged to extend her rule over the whole of the Mediterranean world, in order to fill power vacuums caused by her victories and to defend what she came to possess. By the time of the birth of Christ she was at the head of a vast system of city-states, tributary monarchies and nations, all under her command, *imperium*. She was obliged to defend a vast circular frontier. When the power of Rome passed away, the peninsula reverted to the natural divisions of pre-imperial times.

The fall of the western empire in AD 476 brought about the end of the state, but not of the civilisation. The question which now arose was what would be done by the three great forces still at work in that fallen western world : the vision and the moral power of Rome, the fresh vigour and energies of the new nations, which, though rough, uncouth and ignorant, were overawed by the majesty of Rome and wished to learn from her, and the spiritual forces directed by the Roman Catholic Church, which in very many respects succeeded the Roman *imperium* and transformed and carried on its work in the new circumstances on a new plane. The history of Italy for the next 1,500 years, that is down to the present time, was contained in this situation.

From the fifth century until the end of the eighth, Italy was partitioned between the Goths and their successors : the Lombards in the north and centre on the one hand, and the Roman Emperor of Byzantium, who held the south and the east coast. The popes acquired political power about Rome, and the Moslems conquered Sicily. The main question in this period was whether the Byzantines or the Lombards would gain control of all the peninsula. The popes were averse to both these powers, and settled the matter at the end of the eighth century by calling in Charles the Great and his Franks to dispose of the Lombards and to re-establish the Roman Empire in the west, thus definitively rejecting Byzantine claims. The success of this policy gave the papacy enormous prestige which it used cleverly, wisely and well. The Emperor Charles endowed the popes with lands in central Italy which coincided with the original lands held by the city of Rome in ancient times. The popes remained rulers of Rome and those lands until 1870.

In the meantime Normans liberated Sicily and the south from Islam. Charlemagne apportioned northern and north-central Italy as fiefs of the empire to his vassals. The line of Holy Roman Emperors, whose power was based in Germany, thus acquired rights in Italy which they pursued for the next several hundred years. Both rising Italian city states and the popes opposed their claims, and northern and central Italy became politically divided into the parties known as the Guelfs (anti-imperialist, but not necessarily pro-papalist) and Ghibellines (imperialists, anti-papalists).

The feudal system had the characteristics which are best known in French, German and English history, but it never achieved the development which was so marked a feature in other parts of Europe. The reason was that the ancient cities of Italy enjoyed a very favourable position for trade, both by land and sea, and they soon grew strong enough to oppose the territorial lords and even dominate them. The ineptitude of Charlemagne's successors and the long-drawn-out conflict between the empire and the papacy also weakened the system, and it was already in decline in the eleventh century. Venice, Amalfi, Pisa, Genoa, Milan, Florence and Naples began a period of splendour, and extended their power all over the Mediterranean, especially through the means and opportunities of the crusades. A new form of city organisation—the commune—arose in the north and centre, in Milan first of all. But the south and Sicily remained largely feudal because of the strength of Norman rule and the power of the rival Spanish and French dynasties.

During the period from the eleventh century to the fifteenth Italy enjoyed several periods of renewed spiritual and cultural vitality, early renascences, the best-known of which are the movement begun by St Francis of Assisi in the thirteenth century and the literary movements at Florence and Naples associated with the names of Dante and Boccaccio. And all the time the Church was carrying on its spiritualising work through its monks and priests, the monuments of whose works are the many great monasteries, churches and convents which are among the glories of the country. But politically the peninsula remained in a shattered condition. Its true history was and always has been cultural, not political.

THE RENASCENCE

The communes were transformed into signories during the fourteenth and fifteenth centuries. In other words, they put themselves under strong men—lords—*signori*—in order to be saved from each other's attackers. The Visconti and Sforza duly became dukes in Milan, Rimini was taken over by the Malatesta, Florence by the Medici, Urbino by the Montefeltro, Ferrara by the Este, Mantua by the Gonzaga, and so on. Naples was contested by French and Spanish kings during the whole period and indeed down to the advent of Napoleon. Venice remained a true republic but kept a powerful Doge. In the north-west the counts of Savoy began to expand their power from their mountain home. Imperial power became largely a matter of form; the popes left Italy and went to Avignon. Venice, Genoa and Florence were bitterly competing in the Mediterranean and the Black Seas.

These were the political and social conditions in which the great cultural and artistic movement which we call the Renascence reached its culmination. The city despots were great patrons of the arts, and cultural riches stored in Byzantium began to be transferred to the west; the great schism in the west was healed in 1417, and once more there was a single pope with a clear policy of restoring Rome to her ancient splendours. Generations of great artists, poets, prose-writers, soldiers, musicians, thinkers and scholars suddenly appeared as from a deeply ploughed and sown soil which had been long and carefully cultivated. The Renascence was in many respects a rebirth of that ancient Roman world that seemed to have disappeared into the ground a thousand years before. Now it was enriched with the gains of the culture created by the new peoples during the Middle Ages and the contributions of the tradition preserved at Byzantium. The humanist tradition became a literary one in later centuries, especially in British education, and nowadays most emphasis is placed on its arts, but the earliest humanists were concerned with *living* like Romans and Greeks; that was why they wanted to read the ancient manuscripts.

But the rest of Europe was also growing strong; the Spanish and French monarchies asserted themselves; the new world was discovered between 1480 and 1492. Power shifted westwards. Italy became the jousting-ground of the great powers. The Spanish Hapsburg monarchy eventually defeated its French rival and came to possess Milan and Naples. The popes created a strong State for themselves in the centre. and the Medici family became Grand Dukes of Tuscany. Venice conquered a territory on the mainland, and a number of smaller duchies and principalities became established between Florence, Milan and Venice.

The House of Savoy continued its slow and careful expansion from the north-west. The political situation became fixed from about 1559 until the end of the War of the Spanish Succession in 1715. During all this period Italy remained the cultural centre of Europe. After 1715 the Spanish Hapsburgs were succeeded by their Austrian cousins in Milan and by the Bourbons in Naples and some smaller States. The Medici family became extinct in Florence, and Hapsburgs replaced them in 1737. In 1720 the duke of Savoy obtained the title of King of Sardinia. The great powers continued to fight each other in Italy, but the brilliant culture still contained much vitality, and Italy continued to provide the rest of Europe with every kind of artist, musician, architect and engineer—and two great soldiers, Eugene of Savoy and Raymond of Montecuccoli.

THE RISORGIMENTO

The ideas of the Enlightenment had their effect in Italy in the eighteenth century, but it was the French revolutionary armies which shattered the old order. The political arrangements set up by Napoleon were not so different from what had prevailed before, but they moved Italian minds profoundly and seemed to point towards the dream of a united Italy, freed from foreign domination. When the old order was restored in 1815 it could only be a matter of time before it would be shattered again, this time by Italians. A struggle was begun by liberal and nationalist secret societies against Austrian power in the north and the Bourbon dynasty at Naples. The leaders of the movement were Giuseppe Mazzini, Camillo Cavour and Giuseppe Garibaldi, all men of genius—and most of the time at odds with each other. Cavour gave the House of Savoy political leadership, Garibaldi conquered Sicily and Naples almost single-handed, and Mazzini gave inspiration. After many vicissitudes the Hapsburg monarchy retired from the peninsula. By 1870 the House of Savoy had absorbed all the duchies and principalities and had deprived the pope of Rome and the Papal States. Italy became a single kingdom under Victor Emmanuel II.

Between 1870 and 1914 Italy pursued policies of national uni-
fication, social advancement and colonial expansion, with only
mediocre success in all these directions. In spite of her remaining
claims upon Austrian possessions, she entered into a pact with
Austria and Germany, aimed chiefly against France, with whom
she was in colonial rivalry. But in 1915, on the principle (known
as *sacro egoismo*) that her first duty was to herself, and that this
meant incorporating all Italian-speaking areas, she reversed her
alliances and made war on Austria and Germany. After terrible
struggles she gained her objectives, but the war left her exhausted
and disorientated. Benito Mussolini founded a Fascist Party,
with the aim of restoring the health of the country by corpora-
tive means. The king gave him power in 1922, and he did what
he had promised to do. He turned his government into a dictator-
ship and pursued an aggressive foreign policy aimed at making
Italy dominant in the Mediterranean and finding an empire for
her in Africa. These policies brought him into the power of
Adolf Hitler, and Italy came out of the second world war in a
broken condition on the side of the Allies, against whom she
entered the war. But this experience only stimulated her to the
new effort at national renewal, on democratic lines, in which she
is now engaged.

————

The village of Zoggoneta in the southern province of Foggia,
which has the reputation of being the hottest in Italy. A
typical southern scene.

2

How the Country is Run

ONE difference between the British attitude to government and that prevailing in Italy and other Mediterranean countries is that the object of politics in the latter is felt to be to capture the State itself—not only the government—and through it to lay hold of the whole of society. Another difference, which it may be well to bear in mind at the outset, is that since time immemorial the Catholic Church has taught her people that she is independent of and, in the ultimate analysis, to say the least, superior to the State. The history of Europe has been largely the history of the

Another southern scene, the workers' canteen in a petro-chemical factory at Brindisi. This is a symbol of the State's effort to bring the benefits of modern industrialisation to the south of Italy (the *Mezzogiorno*).

c

conflict set up by this claim. Therefore Italians feel that the State cannot ever be supreme.

The Italian State is a republic. On 2 June 1946, King Humbert II was deposed in a plebiscite by a small majority and the kingdom of Italy passed away. The constitution of the new republic came into force on 1 January 1948. It specifically provides for all the generally accepted liberal democratic freedoms and rights, but also goes on to lay down a series of new rights and privileges for the members of society, not considered as individuals but as members of social groups, ' in which men develop their personalities' (Article 2). It also defines the principles of the State's activity, so covering every sector of public and social life and some relationships which had until then been completely disregarded in constitutional legislation.

There are three main chapters, dealing with (1) Fundamental Principles, (2) Rights and Duties, (3) Organisation of the State. Italy is described as a ' democratic republic founded on work '. There are a Chamber of Deputies of 630 members and a Senate of 315. The deputies are elected for five years by universal direct suffrage, in the proportion of one deputy for every 80,000 inhabitants. There is one senator for every 200,000 of the population, and at least six from every region, besides a few life senators appointed by the President of the Republic, who himself becomes a senator when he leaves office. The President is elected by a joint session of the Chambers and the Senate, together with three delegates from each council of the regions, for seven years. The President has the power to dissolve Parliament, except during his last six months of office. He normally acts in a formal way through his ministers, but the Italian President has never been a mere figurehead, neither did the constitution wish him to be. He is rather like an elected king. He has his own active political staff, makes political moves on his own initiative, requires the prime minister to work closely with him and consults with other party leaders. The last three presidents were active politicians before being elected to office.

The head of the government or prime minister is known as the President of the Council of Ministers. He is not necessarily the

leader of his party, nor even of the strongest party, but is the
man who has been able to gather enough votes from all quarters
to keep him in office for the time being. He is appointed by the
President of the Republic, who has conducted negotiations with
all parties and factions.

The constitution was deliberately made rigid and difficult to
alter, so as to prevent the emergence of governments of the fascist
kind. Fascism was able to carry through its seizure of power in a
perfectly legal manner by means of certain provisions for rule by
decree which existed in the old Royal Statute, but those are excluded from the republican system, except by permission from
Parliament. The President of the Republic appoints ministers on
the advice of the President of the Council. The Council of
Ministers is collectively responsible to both houses of parliament
for its policies and acts, which are laid down in the first place by
the President of the Council.

The ethical, social and economic provisions of the constitution lay down strong safeguards for the family as the basic unit
of society. Education is to be free and untrammelled. The right
to work and the right to receive a just wage for the support of a
family are provided for. Women have the same working rights
as men, due regard being paid to their family duties. Minors are
protected, and provision is made for unemployment, sickness and
disability relief. Trades unions are recognised. Private enterprise
is permitted so long as it does not run counter to the wellbeing
of society or constitute a danger to security, freedom and human
dignity. The same goes for private property. There are provisions
for profit-sharing in industry, participation in management, savings, family housing, and so on.

A Constitutional Court was set up in 1955 with the task of
giving decisions upon the constitutionality of the laws and acts
of the State and the regional governments.

The constitution also provided for regions with their own
parliaments and governments *(juntas)*. So far only five such
regions have been definitely established, but the Government is
now once more going ahead with plans to establish the rest. They
correspond to the old natural geographical and political group-

ings, which existed as separate States practically until 1860. This is one very significant sphere in which, under the Republic, old Italy is reasserting itself against the unitary policies of the Savoy monarchy.

The five regions with autonomous governments are Sicily, Sardinia, Trentino-South Tyrol, Val d'Aosta and Friuli-Venezia. Sicily and Sardinia are separate islands; South Tyrol is German and was part of the Hapsburg dominions until 1918; Venezia-Giulia is largely Slovene, and the Val d'Aosta is mainly French. The adoption of regionalism thus represents a high degree of comprehension and faith in itself on the part of the central government in Rome.

REGIONS AND CITIES

Eight of the twenty regions are in Upper Italy: Piedmont, Val d'Aosta, Liguria, Lombardy, Trentino-South Tyrol, Veneto, Friuli-Venezia Giulia and Emilia-Romagna. They are the richest, because of the abundant sources of hydro-electric energy in the surrounding mountains, the fertility of their soil, their wealth of water supplies, their excellent communications, their more favourable situation in respect to the rest of Europe, in contrast with the south, and because they have always had better government than the south. The capital of *Piedmont* is Turin (1,108,000 inhabitants), a beautiful city with monumental central streets and squares laid out by the dukes of Savoy. It is on the upper reaches of the Po, and today is best known for the huge Fiat motor works and the Savigliano engineering company. It is the site of an international school of technology. Agriculture, especially rice, and pasturage flourish. Good wines are produced in the region, and there are big clothing works at Biella. Other main towns are Asti, Alessandria, Ivrea, Cuneo and Novara.

The *Val d'Aosta* (105,000 inhabitants) has its capital at the ancient Alpine town of Aosta and is geographically part of Piedmont. Since it is mostly French in speech and feeling, however, it has enjoyed a special Statute since 1948.

The capital of *Liguria* is Genoa (848,000 inhabitants). Liguria enjoys an exceptionally mild climate and a remarkably beautiful coastline in the Riviera del Levante, south-east of Genoa. Genoa is a great port, and olives, citrus, peaches and flowers are widely grown. There are big shipyards and engineering works at La Spezia.

The capital of *Lombardy* is Milan (1,675,000 inhabitants), another ancient city and Italy's most important industrial centre. It owes its perennial prosperity to its position on the main trade routes between south-eastern and north-western Europe. It is the financial centre of the country and the site of many great trade fairs. Other large manufacturing towns in the region are Varese and Sesto San Giovanni. Bergamo, Cremona, Pavia, Mantua and Sondrio are other well-known provincial cities in the region.

The region of *Trentino-South Tyrol* (Alto Adige in Italian) consists of the province of Trent joined with the province of Bozen (Bolzano in Italian). The capital is Trent. The province of Trent is largely Italian in speech, but Bozen is German, with an Italian minority introduced after annexation by Italy in 1919. The total joint population amounts to 824,000. There is a strong movement for the two provinces to be separated and for the German population to regain practical autonomy from Italy. The Italian government is disposed to grant most of the claims being advanced, but has not yet done so. The region is notable for its thick alpine vegetation and the mountain scenery of the Dolomites. Agriculture and stockbreeding are strong, and there is enough hydro-electric energy to allow some to be exported. The Tyrolese have a long and interesting history of freedom and independence and possess a remarkably beautiful peasant culture. The region is full of castles.

The *Veneto* covers most of the former mainland territories of Venice, which is still its capital and has a population of 365,000. It has rich agriculture, and Verona is the centre of a vast fruit-growing region. Other main cities are Vicenza, Treviso and Rovigo, all of which have light industries. Padua is famous for its ancient university and for its shrine of the Portuguese Saint Anthony of Padua, a Franciscan friar who died there in the thirteenth century. The country around Vicenza has beautiful villas built by the Venetian nobility, many of them designed by Palladio.

The capital of *Friuli-Venezia Giulia* is Trieste (281,000 inhabitants); it is the most eastern region, lying around the head of the Adriatic Sea and between it and the Julian Alps. It consists of the provinces of Udine, Gorizia, and Trieste and its territory. Like South Tyrol it has a small Ladin minority. Because of its position and the fact that about 500,000 of its inhabitants are Slovene by origin, it also has a special Statute, dating from 1963. Trieste is the natural seaport for a large hinterland in central and eastern Europe.

Emilia-Romagna is one of the great agricultural regions of Italy. The capital is Bologna (483,000 inhabitants), famous for its ancient university, its good food and cooking and its leaning towers. This region is seeking a special statute, but there are resistances to granting one, for fear lest 'Red Emilia' should become too free from Rome. Ravenna, once the Byzantine capital of Italy, now an important industrial city, is in this region. Other cities are Parma and Modena, and Reggio in Emilia.

Central Italy contains six regions: Tuscany, Umbria, the Marches, Latium, the Abruzzi and the Molise. *Tuscany* is the natural centre of communications between the north and the south and the islands. The capital is Florence (455,000 inhabitants) and the beautiful countryside and other cities of art and ancient culture such as Siena, Pisa, Arezzo and Lucca, need no special mention. Modern Tuscany has flourishing agriculture and industry and after Sardinia is the second most important mining area in Italy.

Umbria is the only region which has no coastline. The capital is Perugia (120,000 inhabitants), and other towns are Assisi, Todi, Orvieto, Gubbio, and Spoleto, all famous for their art and cultural and religious associations. There are large steelworks at Terni.

The Marches, of which the capital is the seaport of Ancona (106,000 inhabitants), is one of the most remote parts of Italy, and has many remarkable towns, the chief of which is Urbino.

Besides being the capital of the. whole country, Rome (2,650,000 inhabitants) is also the chief town of a province and the capital of the region of Latium (Lazio). The chief features of Latium's recent history are the rapid growth of Rome, which has now exceeded its ancient population for the first time, and the reclamation of the former wastelands of the Campagna, the Maremma and the Pontine Marshes.

The capital of the mountain region of the *Abruzzi* is Aquila (58,000 inhabitants). The main industries are pasturage and timber, but the interior is declining and losing population. Pescara, the Adriatic port, belongs to it. *Molise* is physically similar to its neighbour the Abruzzi, but has been politically separated since 1965. Its capital is Campobasso (37,000 inhabitants), which is famous for cutlery.

The four regions of southern Italy are Campania, Apulia, Basilicata and Calabria. *Campania* is the region of which Naples is the capital (1,245,000 inhabitants). It has extremely fertile, volcanic soil and intensive cultivation provides a high level of production. Besides agriculture there are flourishing industries of all kinds at Naples.

Apulia extends towards the east and looks out towards Greece and the Levant. The capital, Bari, (340,000 inhabitants) is the site of an important Levant Fair. There is intensive agriculture, and both Bari and Brindisi are important ports for trade to the Adriatic, the Eastern Mediterranean and Africa.

The regions of *Basilicata* and *Calabria* have probably kept more of the old south than any other part, since they are relatively inaccessible, mountainous and harsh, and are largely agricultural and pastoral. The capital, Basilicata, so named because it was for long a province of the eastern emperor, the *basileus*, is Potenza (48,000 inhabitants). Calabria is very mountainous and faces towards Sicily. Its capital is Reggio Calabria (160,000 inhabitants). It has citrus orchards and hydro-electricity plants.

Sicily is shaped like a triangle, and has an area of 9,926 square miles. It is the largest island in the Mediterranean, and has such a mild climate that tropical plants such as sugarcane, bamboo and cotton have flourished there since ancient times. It has also always been celebrated for its corn, vines and citrus. Fishing is important, and so is mining. The capital is the ancient city of *Palermo* (640,000 inhabitants). Sicily has possessed a special statute since 1948.

Sardinia is slightly smaller than Sicily (9,301 square miles). The capital is Cagliari (205,000 inhabitants). The economy is largely agricultural and pastoral, but the State is promoting industrialisation. There are shipping runs between Cagliari, Olbia, Naples, Civitavecchia and Genoa.

The modern regions, now acquiring autonomy, correspond to the old States in the following way : Piedmont and Sardinia the former kingdom of Piedmont; Liguria formerly the territory of the republic of Genoa; Lombardy the territory of the duchy of Milan; the Veneto the mainland territory of Venice; Emilia-Romagna former duchies of Parma, Modena and Ferrara, and the northern part of the Papal States; Tuscany the former Grand Duchy; the Marches, Umbria and Latium, former Papal States; Abruzzi, Molise, Campania, Basilicata, Apulia, Calabria all parts of the former kingdom of Naples and Sicily. Each region will have an assembly, a governing junta and a president.

For direct administration by the central government the country is divided into 91 provinces, each under a prefect, who resides in the chief town. A provincial assembly represents local interests and advises him; he conducts relations with town councils and controls the police, roadbuilding, poor relief, public health, certain public works, and the local agencies of the ministries of State. He is appointed by the Minister of the Interior, and his funds are raised partly from local taxes, loans and revenue from local government property, and partly from general funds.

LOCAL GOVERNMENT

For local government all Italy is divided into Communes (8,050 in 1966), which vary greatly in size and population. Their councils and mayors have the same kind of composition and tasks as have British municipal, borough and rural district councils. A rather notorious feature of local government is that many communes are in very bad financial difficulties. In the first half of 1967, 3,518 of the 8,050 communes had deficits amounting to £54 million. The situation is worst in Sicily and best in the far northern regions. But the communes of the notoriously depressed Molise region, south of Rome, are in as good a position as the northern ones. The commune of Rome has enormous deficits. In Calabria and Sicily electricity supplies have been cut off from whole cities because of non-payment of bills, and employees may receive no pay for months. It is not uncommon for political strife to paralyse local government so much that the central government will appoint a commissioner to take charge.

MINISTRIES

There is a Vice-President of the Council, and, besides the usual ministries found in all countries, such as Foreign Affairs and Justice (in Italy of Grace and Justice), there are a number of other ministries, the exact equivalent of which do not exist in Great Britain. Along with the Treasury, there are the Ministry of Finance and the Ministry of the Budget and Economic Planning (added in 1967) and Ministries for the Reform of the Civil Service, for Industry, for Commerce and Foreign Trade, for Tourism and Recreation, and for State Participation in Industry. This last is of special interest. It has recently attracted attention in Great Britain as representing an alternative to outright nationalisation for State control of industry.

State participation means in effect that the State possesses a controlling interest in a wide sector of industry, but leaves management and the money-market free, subject only to superior State policy. The dynamism of private enterprise is not destroyed; the State ensures that the means of production, distribution and exchange are used for the public benefit. The main instrument of this policy is the system of *Enti Nazionali*—State Corporations—the most prominent of which are The Institute for Industrial Reconstruction—*Istituto per la Ricostruzione Industriale*—IRI, set up in 1933; the State Hydrocarbons Corporation—*Ente Nazionale Idrocarburi*—ENI, and the *Ente Nazionale Energia Elettrica*, set up in 1964. All told there are about 10,000 such *enti*, mostly small and local, but some big, especially in the fields of insurance and transport, and in cinema, opera, and other cultural activities. They are known as ' parastatal ' organisations.

The Italian civil service has the same virtues and failings as bureaucracies the world over. The difference in Italy is that its faults really have been assuming gigantic proportions (delays of seven years in answering a letter and so on), but also that the State has been carrying through reforms. The present minister for this reform proposes to suppress superfluous *enti,* to ensure that civil service salaries shall be competitive with those in private industry, and to decentralise administration in relation with the regions. Certain economic, technical and scientific departments may be erected into autonomous institutions, for the sake of greater freedom and efficiency. Superfluous posts and jobs will be abolished, and mechanisation in office work will be extended. Strict limitations will be placed upon recruitment, and sinecures will be abolished. General standards of recruitment will be raised. As in every country with a certain kind of tradition, the Italian State needed in the past to assert itself in every possible way so as to impress its majesty upon the minds of the citizens, for reasons which have not existed in England for some time, since obedience to the State is automatic in England. A British government office describes itself in its letters as the recipient's servant and sends him a stamped envelope for his reply. In Italy the civil service used to take a lofty tone, and to write to it one has to use official paper upon which a heavy stamp tax is payable. The State does not pose as the subject's servant. This old monarchical attitude is now being vigorously altered.

Besides the ministries, the constitution provides for three organs which have the task of helping in public administration : the National Economic Council *(Consiglio Nazionale dell' Economia e del Lavoro)*, the Council of State *(Consiglio di Stato)* and the Court of Accounts *(Corte dei Conti)*. The first two have advisory functions, which may be binding in certain cases established by law. The National Economic Council (CNEL) has existed since 1957 and consists of fifty-nine representatives of industry and commerce and twenty economic and social experts. The Council of State is the supreme administrative court, and has a president and eighty-six other members with varying functions. It advises ministries on many legal and constitutional matters and also mediates in differences between ministries and various other parts of the administration.

The Court of Accounts supervises the use of public monies. It both sees that government measures only become effective if they conform to law, and examines accounts subsequently to see that no deviations from the rules have occurred. It supervises all matters of public administration in which public funds are engaged, such as pensions and army pay.

POLITICAL PARTIES

Italian government and politics are thoroughly imbued with philosophical outlooks on life, and this was never more true than it is now, when the Government is carrying out a political programme that has its origins in the spiritual and philosophical ideas which its members hold. So economics and particular questions such as higher income standards are always subordinated to the higher purposes of progress in civilisation and culture. The leaders of the Christian Democratic Party never tire of repeating this. The other parties also all have their distinct philosophical systems. The Socialist parties derive largely from Karl Marx, as does the Communist Party. The Liberal Party traces its ideas back to the Enlightenment of the eighteenth century; the Republican Party took its ideas from Mazzini; the Social Movement or Neo-Fascist Party owes its inspiration to the system developed by Mussolini. Only the Monarchist parties lack a coherent philosophical outlook in the British manner. All citizens over the age of twenty-one have the vote.

At the last general elections held in 1963, out of a total of 629 deputies, 260 belonged to the Christian Democratic Party; 166 to the Communist Party; 95 to the Socialist Party; 26 to the

Italian Social Movement. The Social Democrat Party, Liberals and smaller groups, including the Monarchists, returned 87 members altogether. The regional and local elections held in June 1967 confirmed the situation as shown by these figures.

Government has been dominated by the Christian Democrats since 1946. Their party is the successor of the old Populist Party, founded at the beginning of this century and brought to power by Alcide de Gasperi in December 1945. The Christian Democrats are the Catholic Party, drawing on all classes for support and deriving the basis of their strength from the great Catholic masses. They have always been the largest party, but have never been willing (or really able) to govern alone. In the early years of the republic de Gasperi, who proved to be a great statesman, relied for support upon the Social Democrats of Giuseppe Saragat—who separated from the philo-Communist Socialists of Pietro Nenni in 1947—and upon Liberals and Republicans. The eight de Gasperi Ministries between 1946 and 1953 ably supervised reconstruction of the economy, and implemented social improvements along Catholic lines. But that very success led many voters to feel safe in giving their votes to other parties. Communists (led by Palmiro Togliatti) and Socialists gained ground during the period, and de Gasperi himself lost office in an attempt at using electoral manipulation to stop the rising tide. He died, in power again, in August 1954. The next four years were restless ones. The Christian Democrats maintained their predominance, but only by means of help from the dissident Democratic, Socialists and the small parties of the Right. The issues were eventually clarified into whether the government should ' open towards the Right ' or ' open towards the Left '. A right-wing solution with Tambroni as prime minister brought the Left on to the streets. In the end the die was cast by Pope John XXIII, who startled everybody by giving public expression to the widespread feeling that the leftward move—*apertura a sinistra*—was what was needed. Amintore Fanfani favoured this idea, but he was personally unacceptable to the Left, and so the operation was carried through by Aldo Moro, who is still President of the Council in 1967. Pietro Nenni, who had broken off his party's association with the Communists after the Hungarian rising in 1956, is Vice-President, and Giuseppe Saragat became President of the Republic on the retirement of Antonio Segni. The Social Democrats of Saragat and the Socialists of Nenni came to form one single party again in 1967. The right-wing Christian Democrats are out of office but retain power in their party. The main purpose of the coalition is to carry through a programme of social change acceptable to both sides; its second purpose is rigidly to exclude the Communist Party from government and to force it into isolation, where it will shed its subversiveness and be obliged to assimilate to the other political forces operating in the neo-capitalist situation. This policy appears to be having great success. In foreign affairs Fanfani maintains the traditional Italian policy of fidelity to the Atlantic alliance with freedom of action in regard to relations with the East and Italy's special position in the Mediterranean.

RELIGION

It should never be forgotten that the Pope has a casting vote in Italian affairs, to say the least. The Catholic Church enjoys a privileged position in regard to constitutional law, education, family and marriage legislation. The Pope is the Metropolitan of Italy, and the papacy and Italy are clasped in an embrace from which neither can or wants to escape. The Church has been intimately engaged in Italian life from the beginning, and, apart from its spiritual influence, controls very numerous and extensive works of charity, hospitals, schools, universities and colleges. She is a mighty economic power, and in most respects she appears to be more powerful today than she has been for the last hundred years. It is no secret that any pope will intervene in Italian affairs if he believes that vital principles or interests are at stake. In recent years all parties, not only the Christian Democrats, have found it expedient to associate themselves in some way with the moral prestige of the Pope.

The Catholic Church's special constitutional position rests on the Lateran Treaties and the Concordat made with the Italian

State in 1929. There are 54 archbishoprics and 80 other sees, at present being reorganised in accordance with the modern distribution of the provinces and population. 98 per cent of the population is christened into the Catholic Church. There are dissident and Protestant groups, such as the Waldensians in Piedmont, Methodists and Baptists (mainly in the south and Sicily), and Anglican and Episcopalian groups in the big cities, consisting of English-speaking residents. Protestant groups may preach but not proselytise. Some Catholic dioceses in the south and Sicily belong to the Oriental rite. The Salvation Army has a large *Palazzo del Popolo*—People's Palace—in Rome, and publishes a journal called *Il Grido di Guerra*, The War Cry. There are Jewish communities in the larger cities and towns, descending from ancient times and from Jews to whom the popes gave refuge when they were expelled from the Iberian Peninsula.

CURRENCY

The unit of currency is the *lira* (plural *lire*, pronounced lira), which literally means ' pound '. The rate of exchange with the pound sterling ranges from 1,400 to 1,500 according to circumstances. The rate of exchange with the United States dollar ranges from 620 to 625 lire. These ratios are maintained by the Bank of Italy, which also possesses enough gold to cover the note issue. There are metal coins for 5, 10, 20, 50, 100 and 500 lire, and banknotes for 500, 1,000, 5,000, 10,000, 50,000 and 100,000 lire. Notes may not be converted into gold as foreign money, nor exported or imported, except in certain small amounts. Any adverse balance of payments is covered by the very large contributions which tourists make to the Italian economy every year.

TAXATION

The financial year runs from June to July. Public finance is controlled by the Treasury, the Ministry of Finance and the Ministry for the Budget. The regions, provinces and communes also impose taxes. The three most notable marks of the Italian system of taxation up to the present have been prevalence of indirect taxation over direct taxation of income, differentiation in taxes according to classes and sources of income, not simply by amounts, and a high degree of tax evasion. The Government is now engaged in a general reconstruction of the system, in which direct income taxation will take chief place. The indirect tax system, which at present produces more than 70 per cent of all revenue, will be replaced, in accordance with the new methods being adopted in all the Common Market countries, by a tax on added value, together with a selective purchase tax, as in Britain. The new Tax on Added Value *(Imposta sul Valore Aggiunto*—IVA) will replace the old 'tax on general receipts or turnover' *(Imposta Generale sull'Entrata)*, and the above-mentioned indirect taxes which bring in more than 70 per cent of revenue. This IGE has many good qualities from the point of view of the tax-gatherer, but the main objection to it is that it presses unfairly on small producers and organisations to the advantage of the big and powerful ones. The new IVA tax will not fall so much upon turnover as upon the price (or value) added to an article in the course of its movement through the processes of production and the market, in other words, upon the difference between the money spent upon it and the money received for it, with certain reliefs granted to save the tax from amounting to enormous sums in the process. The system was originally worked out in France. The essential difference between the new and the former system is that, whereas the IGE tax was imposed on the *total* value of goods at every stage in production and distribution, the IVA tax will be imposed only on the value *added* at each stage.

That is for the future, however; the present situation is different, and may be described with reference to a few general figures. About 24 per cent of revenue comes from income tax and surtax; 12 per cent from tobacco and spirit excise; 12 per cent from petroleum excise; 25 per cent from the IGE—general turnover or receipts tax—and the rest from extraordinary taxes, such as those for flood relief, lotteries and non-tax sources. This situation may be compared with the British system, in which 50 per cent of revenue is derived from customs and excise taxes on such things as tobacco and spirits, and 45 per cent (at the standard rate of 8s 3d in the pound) comes from Income Tax.

There is a basic distinction in Italian taxation between 'real' and 'personal' taxes. Taxes are imposed individually on income derived from certain specified sources, which come under four heads : (a) movable wealth *(richezza mobile)*; (b) land ownership; (c) ownership of buildings; (d) proprietary farming. Personal taxes are applied to the total income of a person or family, no matter what the source. This is the basis of the central government surtax and the local family tax. The purpose of the distinction is to draw a rough line between income derived from work and income derived from capital. The tax on moveable wealth is the most lucrative of the four for the Government.

The chief local tax is the Family Tax, levied by communes from heads of families in respect of every member of the family. It is progressive over certain ranges and also discriminates between earned and unearned increment. In general there are very marked differences between taxes payable by various social classes and groups with similar incomes derived from earned and unearned sources respectively. A man with an average family, earning about £600 a year, will pay about £33 in taxes;

The Grand Canal at Venice, with the church of Santa Maria della Salute in the background.

a professional man with an average family and an income of about £6,000 will pay about £1,320. British rates are about 20 per cent higher than these.

A characteristic Italian tax is the *Imposta sul Consumo*, levied on foodstuffs entering towns and cities. On wine this was abolished in 1962. Proposed reforms also envisage a property tax and a corporation tax along the lines of the United States one. The general purpose is to increase revenue and lower taxation at the same time, but also to reduce evasion, which is very common. The financial police estimated the proportion of income tax evasion in 1965 to amount to 37.5 per cent. The very rich are taxed so heavily that if they declared their true incomes they would have to pay much more than 100 per cent.

At the beginning of each calendar year the local taxation offices publish lists of the incomes of the richest and most prominent citizens, giving the amount of income declared by them together with the taxation office's estimate of what their incomes really are and the tax payable. However, the Italian taxpayer need not declare interest on bonds or on bank deposits, which are protected by banking secrecy; capital gains by private individuals are not taxed, and the low rate of company tax leads many to set up companies for their private spending. Companies

Treating olive trees at Prima Porta, on the outskirts of Rome. This shows how olive trees are kept in production for hundreds of years; the trunk is hollowed out, so that the sap is forced up the sides to form leaves, new boughs and fruit.

D

carry on endless litigation with the taxation authorities, or keep two sets of books. In the latter case they have to deceive most of their own staff, which means that realistic profit targets may not be set for managers to work for. Foreign firms in Italy, whose true position is known to the taxation authorities of their own countries, are at a disadvantage when it comes to concealing profits from Italian taxation inspectors. However, a new law on taxation of dividends, which forces shareholders to disclose their holdings, also allows non-residents to pay a single withholding tax of 30 per cent on their dividends. Also, those benefiting from a double-taxation agreement between their own countries and Italy will be able to claim refunds of up to two-thirds of the 30 per cent withholding tax.

There is a proposal for reform by which the Tax on Moveable Wealth and the Family Tax will be replaced by a simple, direct personal income tax. The most striking feature of the Italian system at present in comparison with the British and American systems is the multiplicity of taxes payable. This does not mean that taxes are higher—only more irritating. A middle-class office worker may have as many as twenty-six separate taxes to pay. Also, rates are rising continually, whereas in Great Britain and the United States income tax rates are fairly stable. Taxation is not so socialistic in character as British taxation, but it contains some similar features. For example, there are no rebates for the expenses of private education. Finally, the national deficit rose in 1966-7 to about a thousand million pounds sterling. Revenue was expected to amount to about 10,440 million pounds in the same period. (Great Britain 1962-3, £10,224,000,000; 1966-67, £9,838,000,000.)

The Government is concerned not to increase the burden of taxes upon the community, and therefore is prepared to allow revenue to grow less rapidly than in the past. During the years 1959-63 every increase of one unit in the national income was accompanied by an increase of 1.4 in the revenue yield, but it is expected that during the years 1965-9 the increase in revenue in respect of each increase of one unit in national income will amount only to 1.1. Expenditure will also be contained. Savings will be effected by administrative reforms and by keeping the number of government employees within bounds rather than by outright cuts in spending. The administration will need £7,025 million for capital expenses in the five years 1966-70. Of this sum, £3,189 million will be devoted to direct public investment, mainly in public works; £666 million will go to the State Corporations and Industrial Credit Institutes; and £3,270 million will be made available to private enterprise through the Fund for Economic and Social Development. Of the £7,025 million, £2,840 million will be raised on the capital market. The State will be responsible for 46.7 per cent of total public expenditure; local corporations, communes and institutes will handle 15 per cent and social security, insurance and similar organisations will spend 38.3 per cent.

THE ARMY

Italy has been a member of the North Atlantic Treaty Organisation since 1949. The country is at present divided into six military districts. There are five infantry divisions, two armoured divisions, five Alpine brigades and one parachute brigade, as well as various special and support units. Military service is compulsory, and lasts for eighteen months. The public attitude towards military service is a very positive one. The saying *La grande scuola di un popolo è l'esercito*—The army is the great school of a people—has been particularly true in Italy, where military service has been used by the Government as a means of combating illiteracy and bringing men from the various regions of the country together so that they may feel their unity as Italians. There is no public sympathy at all for conscientious objection, which is treated as a civil crime. On the other hand, many young Italians emigrate in order to avoid service. Besides the Alpine brigades, already mentioned, the best known army units are the Sardinian Grenadiers and the Bersaglieri—Riflemen. The latter wear characteristic hats with masses of black cock's plumes. They have a tradition of always advancing at the double and take part in parades at the double.

The core of the regular army is made up of the Carabinieri—Carabiniers—an élite corps, which will be discussed in connection with the police.

THE NAVY

In modern times the Italian Navy has distinguished itself for inventiveness and audacity. It led in the fields of submarines, motor torpedo boats, midget submarines, and frogmen, and exploits carried out with these means against Fiume, Gibraltar and Alexandria, to name only three places, are well remembered. The Navy's two principal tasks are to protect the very long and varied coastlines and to maintain the Italian presence in the Mediterranean at large. Protection is also given to the numerous Italian trawler fleets. Emphasis has therefore always been laid on rapidity and manoeuvrability rather than on weight of fire power and high seas operations.

The main bases are at La Spezia (dockyards), Naples, Taranto and Venice. In 1966-7 the fleet consisted of 3 guided-missile cruisers, 2 guided-missile destroyers, 2 larger destroyers, 5 submarines, 22 corvettes, 74 minesweepers, 13 motor torpedo boats, 5 motor gunboats, 2 anti-submarine patrol boats, 6 landing support boats, 2 surveying vessels and 146 auxiliary vessels of various kinds. There are four commands, each under a flag officer, with the rank of commander-in-chief, at La Spezia, Naples, Taranto and Ancona. In June 1967 a new frigate was launched at Ancona; it is capable of 30 knots and carries 76 and 62 cm guns, rocket-launchers, anti-submarine helicopters, torpedoes and depth charges. A missile-launching cruiser, another frigate, some corvettes and four submarines are under construction, and a further missile cruiser is being planned.

The Navy is also carrying out research on problems of propulsion by chemical and nuclear means, and has recently set up a Centre for Hydrodynamics Experiments. Natives of seaports, fishing ports and the coasts generally are in principle liable for compulsory service of 28 months in the Navy, during which they receive valuable technical and professional training.

THE AIR FORCE

The Air Force has been reorganised since 1951, largely with United States assistance, and is going through the processes of rapid change and modernisation characteristic of all air forces. There are three air regions, with headquarters at Rome, Milan and Bari, with additional commands for Sicily and Sardinia. There are three air brigades, each consisting of 3 squadrons of 25 fighter-bombers, and one air brigade with 2 squadrons of reconnaissance fighters. There are 3 squadrons of interceptor fighters for home defence, 2 of tactical fighters, 3 of anti-submarine aircraft, and 3 of transport aircraft. A perpetual anti-missile patrol is kept up in the northern skies and the air-defence fighter units are supplemented by Nike surface-to-air missiles. The United States Air Force maintains atomic bomb and rocket-launching sites in northern Italy. Modern territorial electronic infrastructures and the new semi-automatic Integrated System for Air Defence are being introduced. The force contains about 60,000 officers and men. Service is for 18 months for conscripts.

The Air Force has recently acquired several new types of aircraft of Italian and United States construction. The new Fiat G-91/Y won a Nato competition for light tactical fighters; it has two turbo-jet engines with a total static thrust of about ten thousand pounds, and can reach a speed of Mach. 0.96, almost the speed of sound. The new Starfighter, known as the Super Starfighter, recently designed in California, will be manufactured under licence in Italy by the Fiat works and subcontractors. The Air Force will acquire 165 of these aircraft, but there has been criticism of the decision, in view of the bad record of the original Starfighter in Germany.

LEGAL AND PENAL SYSTEMS

Italian law is firmly based on Roman law. As was mentioned in regard to the constitution, it has a strong moral cast; many matters which in English custom are regarded as being beyond the scope of law are carefully regulated by the Codes. This is particularly true of family law. There is a Code of the Law of Sport. The existence of Codes does not seem to have reduced argumentation and litigation in any way.

The constitution provides that the judiciary shall be independent and ' subject only to the law '; justice is administered ' in the name of the people ', and the words ' The Law is the same for all ' are inscribed over the bench in all courts. Judges may not be removed from office, and no special courts may be set up.

THE LEGAL PROFESSION

The legal profession is divided into two distinct branches : on the one hand are barristers (*avvocati*—advocates) and on the other procurators (*procuratori*—agents or solicitors) and notaries. There is no fixed distinction between the work of solicitors and the work of barristers, but in general the procurator does the work that a solicitor does in England; he may plead in courts up to Cassation, whereas the advocate pleads in all.

Magistrates and judges are not chosen from among barristers, but belong to a separate branch altogether, organised like the civil service and under the Minister of Grace and Justice (the Keeper of the Seals). A man or woman makes a choice at the outset of his or her career whether to go into ordinary practice or to enter the judiciary. Entrance to this branch and promotion in it are by competitive examination.

The constitution provides for appeals from lower to higher courts. Ordinary jurisdiction is divided into civil courts and criminal jurisdiction.

The lowest grade of civil jurisdiction is that of the Justice of the Peace—*giudice conciliatore*—who may be a professional law officer or be drawn from the community at large as English justices of the peace are chosen. He receives no salary other than his fees, and hears cases involving sums up to 50,000 lire (about £33). The next above him is the Praetor, corresponding to the English Stipendiary Magistrate, with jurisdiction in minor civil matters involving sums up to 750,000 lire (about £450). The next highest is the *Giudice di Tribunale*—District Court Judge; there are 154 of this rank, one in every provincial capital and in about 50 other places. The presiding judge is assisted by two other judges and deals with cases concerned with sums above £400. There are Courts of Appeal in 23 regional capitals, except Aosta, and a number of extra courts of appeal from the *Tribunali*. Appeals may go from these to the Court of Cassation in Rome, which decides on points of law only, not of fact. The highest judicial authority is the First President of the Court of Cassation. Finally there are the Court of Accounts and the Constitutional Court, already mentioned. About 80 per cent of all cases end in the court of the *giudice conciliatore*, whose main task, as his title shows, is to bring the parties to agree with each other rather than to deliver judgment.

CRIMINAL JURISDICTION

The Praetor deals with crimes punishable by fines or imprisonment of up to three years. Appeals from his decision go to a court (*Tribunale*) of three judges; a further appeal may be made to a court of four judges. The courts of first instance for major crimes and felonies are the Assize Courts *(corti d'assise)*, the benches of which consist of three professional and six lay judges (*giudici popolari*), who are roughly equivalent to the English jury but have higher status and judge the facts together with the judge, not separately, as in English law. The Assize Court of Appeal consists of an advisory judge from the Court of Cassation, a presiding judge, an advisory judge from the Court of Appeal, and six laymen. The Court of Cassation (which has four penal sections) deals with final appeals (on points of law, not of fact). The most important cases are held by a full bench (*sezioni unite*) of the Court.

The Procurator General or the ' Public Ministry ' performs the offices performed by the Public Prosecutor, Attorney General and Solicitor General in England. He has the task of protecting the public interest by intervening in civil cases when the matter raises a question of the public good and in starting prosecutions whenever a crime has been committed against the public good (such crimes may be reported by anyone who becomes aware of them).

The constitution establishes a Higher Judicial Council, consisting of the President of the Republic, the First President of the Court of Cassation, the Chief Prosecutor, fourteen representatives of professional judges and seven Members of Parliament. One of this Council's tasks is to watch over the judiciary and provide discipline if needed. The armed services have their courts martial, but crimes committed by servicemen which are not noticed by service law are dealt with by the civil courts.

Changes are taking place in the judiciary system. At the beginning of 1967 it was announced that there were at least two million cases awaiting attention. The Government has shown a wish to make political appointments to the higher courts, and this is meeting with understandable resistance from the judiciary. The Court of Cassation exercises strong control over the judges, not only as regards legal decisions, but also as regards stipends and promotions. There is dissatisfaction with this control and with the control exercised by the Higher Council, changes in the composition of which are being called for. One judge is at present pursuing another through all the courts in the land on a charge of peculation, and there is a general feeling that remedies ought to be found for several maladies, most of which appear to arise from the judiciary's close connections with the State and the fact that it is not recruited from the bar, but is a civil service career.

Italian judges wear a black or red robe and a high black cap, with bands. Barristers wear a black, tasselled gown. Proceedings differ considerably from English ones. The witness is seated in front of the judge, who questions him directly and often intervenes in other ways, arguing with both counsel, witnesses and accused. Displays of rhetoric and emotion are greatly appreciated. In criminal cases the accused is usually kept in a cage to one side of the courtroom. When a case arouses great public indignation it may be transferred to a different city from the one where it would normally be held.

In criminal procedure the accused is first interrogated by a professional investigating judge (*magistrato inquirente*) who is in possession of the information gathered by the police. It is for him to decide whether a prosecution shall be launched, and of what kind it shall be. The rules of evidence are much looser than in English law.

The death penalty is unknown and undiscussed. Perhaps one of the reasons for this is that in Italy most murders are committed through passion and without reflection. Long-planned and carefully-executed murders and other major crimes have been very rare. When they do occur they arouse enormous wonder. The strong bias which English law shows against offences against property is not a characteristic of Italian law, which reflects the attitude that a man has the right to steal if that is the only way by which he may survive. The most notable kind of crime is peculation, especially in public offices or in the many semi-governmental organisations. The prosecutor has the right to ask for a specified term of imprisonment to be imposed on the guilty party, but in practice sentences are never excessively severe (though murder usually results in imprisonment for the term of natural life) and there are many grounds for delays and prevarication. Amnesties are frequent, on religious and national feast days, and it may well happen that a guilty party may not have to spend any time in prison at all, because of delays in bringing on his case, delays in hearing it, amnesties that occurred in the meanwhile, and possible suspension of sentences for a first offence. Italian penal thinking has a definitely liberal character, although purely psychological considerations are seldom taken into account. But an accused person may spend more than a year in gaol before his case comes on, and judicial errors are unfortunately too common.

As in all Roman law, the purpose of a trial is considered to be to discover the facts and the truth of the matter. Besides verdicts of guilty and not guilty, there may also be verdicts of ' release because of insufficient proof '—*per insufficienza di prove*— which is not quite the same as the Scots ' not proven ', and release ' because the act, or fact, does not constitute a crime '

—*il fatto non è reato*. Note that neither of these verdicts gives an opinion about whether the accused is guilty or not guilty, legally or morally speaking.

POLICE

Each city and even each small town or village has its own police force—*Corpo di Vigili Urbani*—The City Watch—Town Watch—which regulates traffic and enforces municipal rules and bylaws. Their uniforms are usually black—white in the summer—and their helmets resemble those worn by English policemen, with the town or city crest and colours upon them. Some towns indulge in quite splendid uniforms for their Watch.

The national police force is the Public Security police—*Guardie di Pubblica Sicurezza*—whose uniform consists of a dark-blue jacket and light-blue trousers, with a peaked cap, and either a black cloak or a greatcoat in winter with a sword for ceremonial occasions. They are under the control of the Ministry of the Interior and guard public buildings, prevent crime and pursue criminals. They have a criminal investigation branch—*la Polizia Giudiziaria*, and also a beach lifesaving service and road patrols, *Polizia Stradale*. Their headquarters in each city is known as the *Quaestura*, under a Quaestor. They are in charge of granting residence permits to aliens and carry out all the normal duties of police forces everywhere. However, they are essentially an urban force, and the countryside in general is policed by the Carabinieri.

Linked with the Public Security police is the force known as the *Celere* (the members are *celerini*), who are riot police and wear a heavy green uniform. They are trained for swift action in emergencies and are equipped with wagons, armoured and mounted with powerful water jets, and armoured jeeps. They spend a lot of time waiting for riots to occur at such places as Parliament House and the United States Embassy in Rome. They were originally organised to fight Communists and became very well known in the years following the war.

The Carabinieri—Carabiniers—are part of the Army; in fact

they are its core, an élite force of 80,000 men, with an admirable spirit and the highest military traditions, and at the same time a truly popular force, enjoying general esteem. For many people, because of their distinctive uniform and dignified demeanour, they must be a symbol of Italy. They have a very strong and yet somewhat equivocal position in the life of the country, because, although belonging to the Army, they act as a police force and perform the functions which the gendarmerie perform in other countries. The force descends from dragoons dating from 1726 but was founded in its present form in Turin in 1824 by the King of Sardinia, and became the main arm with which Piedmontese authority was extended over the whole of the peninsula in the following half-century. They still wear the uniform of the period of their foundation—black swallow-tail jacket, black trousers with broad red stripes, bandolier, cockaded hat, and a voluminous cloak. On ordinary duty a peaked cap is worn, and khaki in the summer, except on ceremonial occasions. They have always been a mounted force. Every village town and city has its Carabinieri, and they patrol every road and street in the country every day. They largely double the functions of the Public Security Police, and are more intensively and extensively organised. For instance, they are on duty in the streets at night when the other police have usually gone off duty, and they run a service of *Pronto Intervento*, with patrol cars, corresponding to the English 999 service. They have their own criminal investigation branch, and it is they who usually make arrests. Carabinieri and police are usually found doing the same things together—such as guarding public buildings and banks and controlling crowds, and it is one of the standing wonders of Italian life that these two rival forces collaborate with such apparent ease and peacefulness. The force has a glorious history of honours won in the field. What it represents for most Italians is best learned from the story of the Carabiniere Salvo d'Acquisto, who was stationed in a village to the north of Rome in 1943. A company of German soldiers was billeted in the village schoolhouse, and during the night someone planted a bomb there. The Germans discovered it, and immediately gathered all the villagers and lined them up, intending to shoot them with machine-guns. Salvo d'Acquisto alone was left aside. He stepped forward and told the Germans that he had laid the bomb (in fact he had not). They immediately shot him and let the villagers go. He was twenty-three years old, and has been described as ' the purest of Italian heroes '. But in the eyes of the Carabinieri he only did his duty.

There are also national forces of Railway Police, Harbour Police, Frontier and Customs Guards—*Guardie di Finanza*— and Forest Police. All cities have their night watch—*Vigili Notturni*—who patrol the streets, making sure that houses and shops are secure and that the streets are safe. The night watch-men at Bari have little trumpets which they sound at every crossroads.

The Public Security police are regulated by a law which also deals with public security in general—for instance, theatre and fire regulations. The law is at present under review, and the changes made will be aimed at reducing the powers of the police over the citizen, especially as regards granting of bail, holding for questioning, and preventive arrest. The last-mentioned is very seldom used, but it is employed, sometimes on a large scale, when the public has been shocked by some crime. Preventive arrest is often followed by enforced residence, that is, a known criminal may either be sent back to his native place and obliged to stay there and report to the police daily for a certain length of time, or be sent to some quite different part of the country, where he may do no harm.

There have recently been suggestions for introducing the death penalty for murders of Carabinieri and policemen committed by bandits in Sicily and Sardinia and by terrorists in South Tyrol.

All Italians are required to carry identity cards, which are issued by the bearer's commune and are valid for ten years at a time. It is no longer necessary for Italians to present their identity cards when signing in at hotels. They may simply give a name and address and no proof is asked for. But foreigners must still present their passports.

3

How they Live

THE basic Italian dwelling-house may be seen anywhere in the peninsula, with regional and local variations; it is built of stone or brick and is usually of two storeys, the upper storey being approached by outside stairs; the ground floor may be used for sheltering farm animals and equipment, and there will be a granary under the roof, or built on to the side of the house. Some houses will have an enclosed yard in the front or in the middle, when the entrance may be through an arched gateway. Farmhouses may be isolated or grouped in various kinds of hamlets and villages, the people going out from these to work in the fields. Roofs are tiled, and two kinds of brick are used in all building: the flat brick, the same as that used in ancient Rome, and the modern hollow brick, used especially today in erecting blocks of flats held together by steel frameworks.

The ancient Latin farm-house had the yard completely enclosed, with the living quarters surrounding it. The central court was known as the *atrium*. Both the villa and the Roman town house grew out of that type of house. The ancient villa was distinguished by its elongated colonnades and several ornamental courtyards, and the town house was the farm-house built in the city, perhaps with several inner courts. The Italian villa, which was developed in Renascence times, is obviously a refinement and enlargement of the typical Italian farm-house, and so is the Italian town house, from which the great houses and palaces of the rest of Europe came to be modelled. If we look at it from the point of view of its origin, we find that it is a very functional construction. The entrance arch leads into the central court, around which lies the ground floor—the *pianterreno*—with stables, coach-houses, stores, offices and a guardhouse. This corresponds to the ground floor of the farm-house, already described. The first floor—*piano nobile*—is the floor upon which the family lives; other floors contain reception and state rooms and bedrooms, and the servants live, or lived, on the top floor under the roof.

All city building in Italy until very recently followed these lines. Buildings were erected as apartment houses, but on this pattern, and this is why Italian cities are full of so many hidden courtyards, in which fountains play and families live quiet lives far from the noises of the street. Nowadays many of the old private palaces—the general word for a city building in Italian is *palazzo*—are not wholly occupied by their original owners, who let out parts as flats, offices and shops. The whole front of the palace of even the grandest family will be occupied, in ancient Roman fashion, by shops. Several branches of the one family, on the other hand, may still occupy their palace on their own, or let out some of it to kinsfolk.

The middle of every old city is made up of dwellings of this kind, standing massively among narrow and twisting alleys and streets where life continues, in spite of the motor car, much as it always was. Basements and shops will be occupied by all kinds of artisans, mechanics, fitters and turners, upholsterers, furniture-makers, carpenters, who live above their shops; all classes live an intensely social life in this age-old way, between the square—the *piazza*—the market, the hostelry—*hostaria*—restaurant—*trattoria*—the bars, and the church, the bells of which punctuate the daily effervescence. The characteristic Italian genius lies precisely in the spontaneous creation of such vital, vivid and well-balanced urban life. Modern urban life is constructed on rather different lines.

A prominent feature in the great economic and social changes of the post-war years has been the rapid and enormous extension of cities by scores of thousands of immigrants from the country-side. Great housing programmes undertaken by the Government resulted in most cities being surrounded by vast new blocks of flats, sometimes known as *isole*—islands. They are not a new phenomenon, for ancient Rome had them too—they were called *insulae*—islands. Both private and governmental agencies built these quickly for cheap letting, and they met the needs of the years after 1949. Development was uneven, because unplanned and uncontrollable. Today there are surpluses of housing in many parts—Rome is said to have 40,000 empty flats—while overcrowding continues in such cities as Naples and in other southern and Sicilian cities. The aesthetic results upon the old cities were deplorable, and Italian society is still struggling to humanise those great concrete mountains where there was no shade and often no modern services. But, although speculation did its damage, there can be no doubt that in general an efficient job of rehousing has been done, and there are innumerable examples of excellent new housing. The chief government housing agency is known as *GESCAL—Gestione Case Lavoratori* —(known until recently as *INA-Casa*—the housing department of the State Insurance Office).

The Government has always favoured ownership by occupiers. The number of dwellings so owned rose from 4,301,000 in 1951 to more than 7,500,000 in 1966. This represents an increase of 76 per cent. The number of families in Italy rose by only 26 per cent in the same period, and therefore, besides the absolute increase in owner-occupied dwellings, there has also been a percentage increase: from 40 per cent in 1951 to 51.5 per cent in 1966. Of people belonging to the richest part of the middle-class, 83 per cent live in dwellings which they own; the figure for the business and entrepreneur class is 72 per cent; for professional men and self-employed workers it is 60 per cent, whereas only 43.3 per cent of clerks or office workers own their own homes, and only 40.7 per cent of ordinary workers. There are about six million dwellings let out for rent; 12 per cent of these are owned by public organisations and 88 per cent by private persons and property companies. Only 12.1 per cent are let at unfixed rents.

By comparison, in Great Britain, nearly 50 per cent of housing, about 9,000,000 dwellings, are owner-occupied, and most of the remainder belong to private landlords. The size of the average Italian urban apartment is about the same as the British one (930 square feet). In 1966 72,876 dwellings were built in Italy. The figure for Great Britain in the same year was 88,149.

Housing construction is at present in a crisis, owing to the over and uneven development already mentioned, and to the fact that the Government maintains rents at rates fixed during the period of acute shortage. Building activity has declined by 40 per cent a year in recent years, and the builders are pressing the Government to free the market. The number of new houses amounted to 341,000 in 1965, but only 259,000 in 1966.

By a law of 1 November 1965 the government lent housing societies up to three-quarters of the cost of building. The average cost of an apartment is about £5,000, and loans of three-quarters are available from housing societies at $5\frac{1}{2}$ per cent; they are repaid at the rate of about £20 a month. This arrangement is commonly regarded as too burdensome and unsuccessful. But outright renting would cost almost twice as much.

The Government's plans for housing take note of the fact that

---

The quarter known as the E U R (*Esposizione Universale di Roma*) at Rome is a modern quarter on monumental lines, mainly housing Ministries of State. In the centre of the photograph is the Ministry of Foreign Trade.

The Quirinal Palace at Rome. It was built in the sixteenth and seventeenth centuries and was the usual and favourite residence of the popes as rulers of Rome. Then it became the royal palace under the Savoy monarchy. Today it is the residence of the President of the Republic. The figures of Castor and Pollux flanking the obelisk are attributed to Phidias and Polyclites.

too much ' luxury ' building was done in the past and that one result has been that costly flats stand empty while workers cry out for flats. It proposes to make a big increase in the State's direct contribution to housing finance, amounting to about 25 per cent of all costs. Finance will be supplied on two planes—for subsidised housing and for ' assisted ' housing; the former for workers' dwellings, the latter for private building. The new laws on city planning will also help to ensure that land is available at reasonable prices, protected from the evil results of speculation.

Living apart in a cottage or enclosed house of one's own is not an Italian ideal. Italians like to live together in the large blocks of flats which are now the most striking feature of all modern cities. One great advantage of intensive housing construction is that it restricts the tendency for cities to spread unmanageably. The Italian worker generally does not have to go so far to work as the average British worker, he is in closer touch with his home and he can perhaps return there for his lunch and siesta if he wants to. The sharp distinction between residential and business and working districts, so characteristic of Anglo-Saxon cities, is non-existent, except in Milan, or at any rate is far less marked. All parts of the cities are thus generally fully alive all the time. There

Masterpieces of art are commonplace in the streets and squares of Italian cities. This is a view in the Piazza della Signoria at Florence, with Michelangelo's *David*.

E

are modern residential quarters, with villas and *villini*, and there are some outlying residential suburbs and garden cities, but suburbs are as a rule unknown, and modern urban life tends to take on the characteristics of the old urban life described earlier. The centre of the city-dweller's existence is not a suburb but his quarter, the *quartiere*, which has all the characteristics of a highly populated village within the great city, which itself tends to turn into a number of villages through these quarters (also called *rioni, contrade*, etc.). City government has so far been centralised, but there are moves to decentralise it into the *rioni*. The chief danger to the Italian sense of a living city is imported ideas about zoning and planning, which have lethal effects. The new quarters are now struggling to create their own individual lives and characters. One hindrance to this is that during the rush to build anything anywhere, very little space was left for squares, gardens and playing fields. The general tendency is always towards overcrowding and inadequate services, but even these things can have good social effects, unknown to planners.

In modern housing and building generally the traditional courtyard-centred plan has lost ground, but there is a great deal of brilliantly-conceived modern domestic architecture, especially in such quarters as the EUR garden city in Rome.

An interesting and novel phenomenon is that, as the movement from the countryside to the cities continues and agricultural methods change, abandoned farm-houses are being bought up by city-dwellers and renovated into villas as holiday and weekend resorts. Another result of recent development is that housing and residence are taking on class characteristics. In the older parts of the city all classes live side by side, as in the older parts of London; but now workers' flats are built on one side of a city and flats for the rich on the other. This tendency is being resisted.

MODERN CONVENIENCES

The most salient feature of the interiors of all Italian dwellings is the use of marble. Timber is relatively rare. Since winters are short, Italian houses were once notoriously ill-heated. Fire-places are few, and a favourite means of heating was a large brass brazier, set in the middle of the floor and carried from room to room. Such braziers were also carried on the arm, and the smell of burning charcoal used to be one of the sweetest smells of Italian cities. Nowadays stoves and central heating are pretty well the rule, like shutters and Venetian blinds (known as *persiane*—Persian blinds). Kitchen furnishings were rather scanty until recently. A rather old-fashioned style of furniture is still made and preferred, but advanced styles in excellent taste are to be found everywhere.

All kinds of modern conveniences—washing machines, vacuum cleaners, mixing machines and so on—are now common and are known as *elettrodomestici*, ' electric servants '.

SERVANTS

Human servants are rarer than they used to be, but not so rare as in Britain. Domestic service is still regarded as an honour-able calling, and the State has made laws to improve the lot of servants considerably in recent years.

The household of a Roman marquis may still have from fifteen to twenty servants, coming from his estates. Country girls begin life in the city by becoming the maid of all work, *tuttofare*, or the nurse, *bambinaia*, in a middle-class house. A feature of this situation is that many Italian families now engage English girls to look after their children. The position used to be the reverse.

WHAT THEY EAT AND DRINK

The staple food of all Italy is *pasta*, a dough, including eggs, made in multitudinous forms, of which macaroni and spaghetti are only two. It is made from the flour of a hard variety of wheat, and is best made every day at home. But there are shops every-where in which the main varieties are prepared fresh every day.

Two main meals are eaten each day. The peasant and working man will have a substantial breakfast of bread, bacon, perhaps cheese and coffee. An ordinary sedentary city dweller will take a raw egg and a small cup of black coffee, or milk coffee and stale bread left over from the day before, or he will go to a bar on his way to work and have a *cappucino* or *caffe latte* with a sweet roll, brioche or piece of pastry.

The midday meal *(pranzo)* is taken about two o'clock. Most middle-class people go home for lunch or eat in a restaurant. A middle-class family will eat hors d'oeuvres, pasta, and some kind of meat or fish dish (veal or perhaps a steak), a vegetable dish (known as *contorno*, ' surroundings '), salad, cheese, a sweet, fruit and coffee. Each dish is served and eaten separately.

Simpler families eat a great deal of beans, lentils, chickpeas and many other kinds of grain and flour dishes. Meat used to be very rarely eaten, but since the Government now imports supplies from South America it has become much cheaper and more common.

The evening meal (*cena*—supper) is taken about eight or nine o'clock, or later in some places (in the south both lunch and dinner are eaten much later than in the north). A broth or vegetable soup may take the place of pasta, but the rest of the meal will follow the pattern of the midday meal, which is the main one of the day. The wine, drunk at all meals, is usually the wine of the district, and can be bought very cheaply. Beer is being drunk more and more, but not with family meals so much as in restaurants.

Cooking in Italy, like everything else, is regional and local rather than national. There is no such thing as ' Italian cooking ', just as there is no such thing as ' French cooking '. There is Venetian cooking, Roman cooking, Neopolitan and Genoese cooking, and so on. Meat is becoming more important than it used to be, as has been said. Tuscany is noted for its good beef. Since all parts of the country are fairly easily accessible from the sea, fresh fish is obtainable everywhere; shellfish, octopus, swordfish and eels are all great favourites. Stockfish, anchovies, sardines, salted herrings and tunny are very common. The main condiments are olive and seed oil, garlic, and every kind of herb and spice, freely used. Black and green olives, mushrooms, artichokes, and red and green peppers are very much liked. Italians eat many more parts of animals than is now customary in Britain. There are many kinds of excellent hams and sausages, and all kinds of very tasty and interesting dishes, pastries and sauces, prepared and eaten by all classes. The menu of a good and cheap Roman restaurant, run by a family from the Abruzzi mountains near Rome, lists the following main dishes : *Bocconcini di vitello*—veal stew; *Saltimbocca alla romana*—braised veal with bacon and rosemary in a sauce (*saltimbocca* means ' jump into your mouth '); *assobuco*—veal shanks stewed with peas or mushrooms; *abbacchio*—roast lamb; *bistecca di maiale*—pork chop; *bistecca di manzo*—beefsteak; *pollo alla cacciatora*— chicken roasted and fried in herbs; *trippa alla romana*—tripe in the Roman way; *carcioffi alla romana*—artichokes. Dandelions, fennel, endive and various kinds of grasses and weeds cut by old women from the roadsides are used in salads, besides lettuce.

There are many kinds of sweet cakes, and hundreds of cheeses, the best-known of which are Bel Paese from the north, Gorgonzola, also from the north, Cacciocavallo—' horse cheese '— from Sicily, Parmigiano, used on pasta, Pecorino, from goats' milk, Provolone, Ricotta and Stracchino, cottage cheeses.

All cooking is based on the regional products, so what is available in Rome may not be available in Naples. Bologna and Florence have reputations for the best food and cuisine in all Italy, but it would be possible to write volumes on all the dishes to be found in each region and province. More rice is eaten in the north, and fish dishes are naturally more abundant all around the coasts. Kid (*abbacchio*) is a Roman speciality. *Lasagne* and *sugo Bolognese* are characteristic of Bologna. Various kinds of dish are eaten on certain feast days : the paschal lamb on Easter Day at Rome, and roast pork on St John's Day are two examples. On St Joseph's Day one eats a kind of fried cake, the *bigne di San Giuseppe*, and so on. A feature of city life is *rosticcerie*, cookhouses, where such dishes are sold over the counter to be eaten on the spot or taken away.

The wine of the place may be ordinary wine (*vino sciolto*) or bottled wine of a better quality. There are very many Italian wines, and a great variety. Very few approach the qualities of the best French wines, but many have good characters. Chianti, the best-known comes from a *small* hillside in Tuscany. Wines from Burgundian stocks—Pinot, Cabernet, Gattinara, Merlot—are produced in Piedmont and on the hills of Lombardy and the Veneto. South Tyrol has several good red and white wines: Kalterersee, Eppian and Traminer. The well-known red Valpolicella is grown near Verona, and Lambrusco belongs to Bologna. Sparkling wines are produced around Asti in Piedmont, and a good dry white wine known as Verdicchio is produced in the Marches.

The wines of the north and centre are generally heavier and inclined to be slightly effervescent, in comparison with those of the south. The well-known wine of Rome is Frascati, a somewhat liquory white wine. Further south come Falerno and Cecubo, modern descendants of the ancient Falernum and Caecubum. Tuscany produces the celebrated Est! Est! Est! Various light, excellent reds and whites grow from the lava of Vesuvius and on the isle of Capri. Cirò is an excellent wine from the Basilicata. Sicily produces several good wines from French stocks. Apulia and other parts of the south produce lower grades in large quantities. In the south red wine is known as *vino nerọ*, black wine, and one does indeed find wines that are almost black or a very deep purple. Sardinian wines are also much appreciated.

HOW THEY SPEND THEIR MONEY

The cost of living in Italy rose by 2.3 per cent in 1966, but at the same time earned incomes showed a general increase of 7.4 per cent: 3.6 per cent in agriculture, 7.3 per cent in industry and 8.1 per cent in the professions. This continued and spreading prosperity is causing notable changes in Italian spending habits. Until the present economic advance set in, the great majority of Italians, and not only of the working classes, had to spend most of what they earned on the immediate necessities of life. Today the case is different. The trades unions have not been slow to press for greater shares for the workers, with what has been described as ' giddy success ', insisting that all increases in both national income and the cost of living should be accompanied by wages and salary increases, in accordance with the *scala mobile*—the escalator principle or sliding scale. The industrial population is well paid, and the economy is moving towards becoming a consumer economy, living on its own momentum so to speak. A study conducted by the Bank of Italy in 1966 stressed the importance of the family in the Italian economy and pointed out that twelve or fifteen million families own almost all the national wealth either directly or indirectly, and that three-quarters of the demand in the country for goods and services comes from them. The sector of private consumption therefore has vast importance in the national economy. This contrasts with the case in Britain, where only 54.3 per cent of national expenditure comes from consumers' spending.

In 1966 private expenditure of residents in Italy amounted to £15,000 million at current prices. Of this sum something approaching 43 per cent was spent on food and drink. There is a slight tendency for this proportion to be reduced in favour of more general private expenditure, on housing, shoes and clothing, transport, hygiene and health, recreation and culture, in that order of importance. No less than £520 million is spent on tobacco every year, and this is almost as much as is spent on fuel and electricity. A great deal (about £500 million a year) is spent by new couples on setting up households, but the number of marriages per year is declining noticeably (417,000 in 1964, 385,000 in 1966).

Though the cost of living increased by 2.3 per cent in 1966 and there was an overall increase in incomes of 7.4 per cent, private spending increased by only 5.7 per cent on the previous year. This shows that savings are being made, but also that demand is not keeping up to production in the field of private consumption.

Only about 5 per cent of income is spent on household labour-saving machines. The motor car has now become a chief expense item and most cars are kept for convenience and pleasure. In 1966 there were 6,322,398 motor cars on the roads in Italy. These represent an average of about one car to every two families. There is no cult of old cars, and Italians sell the old car and buy a new one on the average every five or six years.

A large proportion of consumer spending is now done by the unmarried young. The peasantry is largely self-sufficient, and its spending is for the most part concerned with equipment and services. The young of the new industrial populations, however, are the mainstay of consumer industries—soft drinks, records (upon which, however, they spend only 2 per cent of their total expenditure), cosmetics, the cinema, record-players. They spend 22 per cent of their incomes (which average about £25 a month) on clothing; 35 per cent of them give all their earnings to the family, 45 per cent give a part, and 20 per cent keep all that they earn. They save almost nothing.

MEDICAL SERVICES

Europe owes its medical science, like so much else, to Italy. The first medieval school of medicine was founded at Salerno in the tenth century. Then Bologna became the chief medical school of Europe, and every medical textbook contains many terms deriving from the work and names of Italian physicians and surgeons. Today Italy has many great hospitals and renowned medical centres at Rome, Padua, Milan and Bologna, to name the best-known.

Features of Italian provincial life are the district midwife and the *medico condotto*, the doctor employed by the commune to give his services free to those on the poor list. Today private practice is becoming more and more difficult, and most doctors find it necessary to belong to one or other of the insurance schemes or to have a connection with an insurance company. The Ministry of Health controls all State medical and health services, working through local offices and bodies.

Medical expenses are fully covered in almost all cases by means of a large number of insurance schemes and insurance companies, funds and corporations, such as the *Istituto Nazionale di Previdenza Sociale*, INPS, which dates from 1898, and the *Istituto Nazionale di Infortuni sul Lavoro*, INIL, which dates from the Fascist period. Insurance for medical benefits is already almost universal (covering 85 per cent of the population) and in some cases compulsory, according to the industry. The Government now proposes to bring all the various medical benefit schemes under one control, the National Health Service— *Servizio Sanitario Nazionale*. Private clinics and hospitals will be able to carry on as before, and so will private medical assistance schemes.

HOSPITALS

A feature of the hospitals of Italy is the great number which are run by the Catholic Church. On the other hand a great proportion of nuns are employed in State hospitals, side by side with lay nurses.

The rapid increase in national income has not been accompanied by an equal increase in hospital services. Some hospital buildings are more than 200 years old and there is considerable overcrowding. The Government plans to spend £200 million on new hospitals in the next five years and £33 million on local health centres. The problem of hospitals in Rome may be taken as typical of all big cities in the country. Rome has a population of virtually three million and an area of about 450,000 acres. It is considered that there should be 13 hospital beds for every 1,000 of the population. The need is therefore for 39,000 beds, but in fact there are only from 27 to 28,000. The number of persons brought to hospital per 100 of the population has almost doubled since 1955. In 1965 beds in one of the biggest hospitals (the Santo Spirito hospital, founded by Anglo-Saxon kings) were in use to 100.02 per cent of capacity, whereas in theory and law only 80 per cent of beds should be in use at any one time. The situation is worst in mental hospitals.

The shortage of nursing staff is very serious. The lowest number of nurses per 1,000 of the population necessary to ensure efficient care is 50. The figure for Italy is actually 13.5 per 1,000 inhabitants, in strong contrast with that for Great Britain, which is the ideal one of 50 per 1,000. The Ministry of Health would like to have the same proportion, and various reforms regarding studies, nursing certificates and conditions of work are being introduced for this purpose.

Ambulance services are run by the Red Cross Society.

SOCIAL SECURITY

The situation as regards social security has so far been similar to that of medical benefits. It has been in the hands of private and State assurance companies, and the Government is now making plans to provide a general social assurance scheme, bringing all the various organisations under a single control, which will also administer the already-existing invalid and old-age pensions. Such pensions are many and varied, but are generally paid at very low rates (the old-age pension amounts to £7 to £14 a month). The aim is to provide a minimum of £12 a month by 1967 and £14 after that, and also to widen the scope of the present pension laws.

Family allowances are paid, but at present only to town and city dwellers. By 1968 they will also be paid to the various classes of peasant (£15 a year for each child up to the age of fourteen, and also for children continuing their studies up to the ages of twenty-one or even twenty-six). Allowances are paid for old parents as well as children.

In general the family takes care of its old people (and the old people take care of the family's young people!). For those old people who have no families there are many homes, such as those run by the Little Sisters of the Poor and other orders of nuns and monks. There are also many homes for particular classes of old people, such as the Giuseppe Verdi Home for Musicians in Milan, founded by Verdi himself.

There are many orphanages, such as the Martinitt Boys' Orphanage in Milan, founded in 1532 by the Venetian saint Jerome Emiliani. Today there are also 28 *enti* operating for the care of children and adolescents. The *Opera Nazionale*

Maternità ed Infanzia runs child welfare centres and kinder-gartens in every part of Italy, and the Italian Red Cross Society does the same kind of work as in other lands. It takes a special interest in the problem of spastics and the rehabilitation of the physically handicapped generally. The charitable institutions of all kinds run by the Catholic Church in all parts of the country are too numerous to mention. They far outnumber lay organisa-tions doing similar work.

4

How they Work

UNTIL about 1930 Italy was a mainly agricultural society. Since the war it has changed from an agrarian, overpopulated and poor country into a fast-growing urban, industrial society. Agriculture contributed 32 per cent of the gross national product in 1950, but only 22 per cent in 1960, and it will contribute only about 13 per cent by 1970. Most of the rest comes from trade and industry. In the years 1957-67 Italian industrial production increased by 91 per cent. It has increased 300 per cent since the war and 1,000 per cent since the beginning of the century. Yet Italy is not naturally endowed with raw materials suitable for creating an industrial system and has to import large quantities. The reasons for the present development lie in financial factors, the ability and inventiveness of the people, the country's geographical situation for trade with Africa, the Middle East and Eastern Europe, and its relation with the European Common Market. The industrial revolution which it is experiencing differs from the industrial revolution experienced by England in the last century. The English industrial revolution was practically an unconscious event, without precedents, which did immense harm to England. The capitalism which is directing the Italian industrial revolution is late capitalism, and is being consciously controlled by a government which has other than purely economic goals in mind : it is concerned above all with cultural and social values.

The revolution therefore means something very different to Italians from what it meant to the English people; it has come as an exciting and liberating adventure, full of great promise, releasing all kinds of powers and potentialities. The first industrial revolution brought manifold horrors to the masses of the north of Europe. The new one means property and ease for millions of Italians for the first time. The factories in which they work are almost all new, and they are taking to living in vast colonies about them.

ELECTRICITY

In 1938 Italy had an installed capacity of 15.8 million kilowatts and production stood at 15,500 million. Losses due to the war were fully made up by 1947, and by 1954 output was roughly double that of the pre-war period. By 1960 production capacity of *new* plant amounted to 12,580 million kWh. About 85 per cent of output comes from water sources and about 70 per cent is used by industry. Until 1964, 75 per cent of capacity was nominally in private hands, but the State gained a controlling interest in most companies through the Industrial Reconstruction Institute, and then, by a law of December 1962, set up a national electricity authority—*Ente Nazionale Energia Elettrica*, which has taken over almost all thermal and hydro-electric plants (these numbered 1,040 in December 1966).

In 1966 total production of the ENEL amounted to 60,373 million kWh. Energy was supplied to 20,206,766 customers, an increase of 4.8 per cent over the number of users in 1965. Most customers are householders and shopkeepers. Six new plants were installed during the year, adding a total average annual potential of 248 million kWh. Forty-five new transmission lines were erected over 600 miles. An interesting achievement in this regard was the installation of a submarine electric cable between the mainland and Sardinia, with remote control. About 2,700,000 new installations in customers' premises were made during the year.

NUCLEAR ENERGY

Nuclear energy provides about 6.4 per cent of total production of electrical energy at present. There are three active nuclear powerhouses, at Latina, Garigliano and Trino Vercellese, and a fourth will double present supplies. Italy therefore comes third after the United States and Great Britain as a producer of nuclear energy, but fourth when the USSR is taken into account. Fourteen more nuclear power stations are to be built in the next fourteen years. It is expected that demand for electricity will increase by about 9 per cent a year for the next few years, and funds are being put aside to provide new plant to meet these eventualities. The ENEL finances itself from its charges and from public and State loans.

Its tariffs have remained static since 1959, and as costs of production have risen considerably since then, this actually means that consumers have benefited from a lowering of real prices, even after nationalisation. (Prices of electricity in Britain rose by 1.85 per cent after nationalisation and have risen by 12 per cent since 1959). The favourable situation has been possible in Italy both because of improvements in administration and general efficiency and because the number of consumers has been constantly rising.

PETROLEUM

The discovery of oil and gas had great psychological as well as economic effects, especially in view of the fact that there is a natural limit to the development of hydraulic supplies of energy —about two-thirds of the potential has already been brought into exploitation. The first oil found in commercial quantities was at Cortemaggiore (together with gas). The story of the development of these sources is inseparably connected with the name of Enrico Mattei and the AGIP petroleum company. Mattei became the president in 1953 of a new State agency, the National Hydrocarbons Board—*Ente Nazionale Idrocarburi*—which holds controlling interests in prospecting, production and distribution companies. A new law on petroleum passed in 1956 gave the ENI exclusive rights in the Po valley, but allowed other concerns to compete with it in the rest of the peninsula and Sicily. Several of these other concerns are financed from the United States (Petrosud and Gulf Italia). Most oil is now found in Sicily (at Ragusa) and there are about 2,000 wells now in production all over Italy, producing about 2.3 million tons a year, which amount to about 4 per cent of national requirements. The refineries have a capacity of about 100,000,000 a year, and therefore they keep themselves in operation by importing large quantities of crude oil and exporting its derivatives. There are now about 1,250 miles of oil pipelines in the country and a second transalpine pipeline is being constructed.

In 1966 internal consumption of petroleum products amounted to 45 million tons, but for the reason mentioned above, imports are much higher (79,200 million tons in 1966). The sources of Italian petroleum imports are very varied. The biggest suppliers are Kuwait (33.8 per cent), Saudi Arabia (21.4 per cent), Iraq and Lybia (10.9 per cent each). Abui Dhabi and Qatar provide 2 per cent and the Soviet Union 9.8 per cent. The last source is perhaps the most interesting, both for political reasons and because there is a project to build pipelines from Kiev to Trieste, for transporting petroleum and gas from the Baku fields.

The great Middle East crisis of 1967 proved the wisdom of the ENI policy of the greatest possible diversification of its sources and spurred it on to seek even greater variety. The law requires that reserves of two months be kept to meet any interruption of supplies, and in this case there was no need to draw on them, or to put prices up.

The Government is now proposing to grant the ENI exclusive rights to search for oil and gas in the Mediterranean Sea and on the Italian continental shelf, and is going ahead with plans to build more pipelines, so as to free the roads from oil-tankers. The uses of petroleum and its numerous products and by-products are the same in Italy as in Great Britain, but there is much greater use of methane than at present in Britain.

METHANE

The first gas fields were discovered, after many empty years, by the AGIP company in 1945, at Caviaga, Ripalta, Cortemaggiore, Cornegliano, Bordolana, Correggio, Ravenna, and Catania. By 1954 it represented 10 per cent of all energy produced and was saving imports of 5 million tons of coal. This industry is also controlled by the ENI. There are centres of production all through the Po valley from Milan to Ravenna, others in many places down the east coast and in Basilicata, and at Catania, Gela and Ragusa in Sicily. Production in the north is already insufficient to meet demands, which are expected to double by 1980. The existing 3,300 miles of gas pipelines (mainly in the Po valley to which Genoa is linked) will be extended to about 5,600 miles by about 1980—in the north, in Tuscany, down the east coast, in Latium and Campania, throughout the south and Sicily—and will about double present consumption. In order to meet this demand, the ENI is going to look for methane off the Sicilian and Adriatic coasts (it was the first firm in Western Europe to discover marine deposits of methane). It is also taking part in exploration of the North Sea for gas and oil, with notable

----

Italy comes third in the West for production of nuclear energy, after the United States and Great Britain. This is a view of the nuclear centre at Frascati, in the Alban Hills near Rome.

Italy is now becoming an industrial nation. The special Italian industrial talent is for precision and other products which involve craftsmanship and individuality, as in this aircraft factory at Turin.

success, and has sent drilling platforms to the Red Sea and the
Persian Gulf, in both of which finds have been made. Methane
will be imported into Italy both by land and sea. The first imports
will come from Libya. The ENI has already constructed a big oil
and gas pipeline from Genoa to Ingolstadt in Germany; this is
625 miles long and has a capacity of 18 million tons a year.
Another will run to Ingolstadt from Trieste.

Methane is chiefly used for raising heat in industry, thermal
electricity, domestic cooking, road transport, and as a fuel and
a raw material in the synthetic rubber industry. Some petrol is
also got from it. Bottled gas for domestic purposes is mainly used
in stoves and heaters, and has proved of great benefit to peasant
households. Cities and towns are now introducing it into their
normal supplies.

MARBLE

Marble quarrying is a special Italian industry, carried on
chiefly in the enormous masses of marble that are the mountains
above Massa-Carrara near the coast of Tuscany. The quarries
were once honoured by the presence of Michelangelo himself,
who came to cut out and select his marble. Exports go from

Fishermen at Naples hauling a catch on to Via Caracciolo.
Such mingling of simple life with modern sophistication, represented by the motor cars, is characteristic of Italy and one
of the reasons for its perennial vitality and charm.

In the rice fields of Piedmont. Rice was known in Italy in
ancient times, but modern cultivation of it is due to Count
Camillo Cavour, the architect of modern Italy. The country
now produces all it needs, and rice rivals pasta as a staple dish
in the north.

Ceramic workers at Chianciano, near Siena in Tuscany. The
crafts flourish in most parts of Italy and most cities have
hundreds of workshops such as this, where old traditions of
life and work are as strong as ever.

F

there to all over the world, and several English firms have offices or agents in the town of Carrara.

MINERAL RESOURCES

The main minerals produced by Italy are iron, lead, zinc, manganese, bauxite, mercury, sulphur and pyrites. Most lead and zinc come from Sardinia; mercury and sulphur come mainly from Sicily and Tuscany; Italy provides the world with more than a third of its supply of mercury. Half the Italian production of aluminium is at Mori and at Bozen, from bauxites mined in Apulia; the rest is produced at Borghofranco d'Ivrea in Piedmont and at Porto Maghera. Most of the iron comes from Sardinia and Tuscany (Elba and the mainland opposite, near Piombino).

In general, however, production of minerals is quite inadequate to needs, especially those of rapidly-growing modern industry, and large imports are needed of iron, steel scrap, iron ore, pig iron and coking coal.

IRON AND STEEL

Industry grew up and developed first in Lombardy and Piedmont. The almost complete absence of coal for coking made development difficult before the war. Wartime destruction gave the opportunity for reconstruction, the main points in which were that less dependence was placed on supplies of scrap metal and a greater balance was achieved by expanding blast furnace capacity. Coastal sites at Piombino, Bagnoli, Civitavecchia, and Cornigliano, near Genoa, were chosen for further expansion, in view of the fact that supplies come by sea. A big new plant is in operation at Taranto. These and the majority of other plants are owned by the Finsider group, which is a subsidiary of the IRI (Industrial Reconstruction Institute), and therefore an instrument of the State. Other smaller plants are situated at Turin, Monza near Milan, Bergamo, Brescia, Terni in Umbria, Aosta and Trieste. Stress has naturally been laid on the use of electric furnaces, in which field Italy leads in Europe. The Finsider works mainly through the company known as Italsider, which in 1966 produced 95 per cent of all pig iron, 52 per cent of steel, 49 per cent of sheet metal and 60 per cent of tin plate and galvanised iron. It employs about 39,000 persons. The total labour force in the whole industry numbers about 110,000.

In 1966 production figures for the iron and steel industry were as follows. Pig and cast iron 6,257,027 tons; steel 13,611,765 tons; sheet steel 10,305,202 tons; sheet iron 74,061 tons; iron alloys etc. 158,759 tons. The IRI expects that by 1969 it will be possible to produce 8.3 million tons of cast iron, 10.5 million tons of steel and 9.3 million tons of finished products.

ENGINEERING INDUSTRIES

The heavy and light engineering industries, which depend on the steel industry for their production, are the basis of the whole economy, since they produce machines for other manufacturing industries, for services and for transport. Perhaps the success story of Italian industry is most brilliant in this field. Production indexes are enormously higher than those of 1938. Heavy engineering is naturally situated near the main steelworks, especially near the coast, and, once more, the State plays a big part through the IRI subsidiaries Italcantieri (shipyards), Finmeccanica (mechanical engineering), Stet (telephones), Finmare (maritime transport), Alitalia (air transport) and Rai-Tu (radio and television).

SHIPBUILDING

The main shipbuilding ports are Genoa and Trieste, Naples, Monfalcone Castellmare, La Spezia, Ancona and Venice. The Italian merchant navy lost 88 per cent of its ships during the last war, so the shipbuilding industry received a great call upon its energies directly afterwards. Some of the best known dockyards are those of the Ansaldo company at La Spezia and Genoa, which built a number of transatlantic liners such as the *Michelangelo* and the *Andrea Doria*. The naval dockyards at Ancona, Naples and La Spezia have also been kept busy re-equipping the Italian fleet. Italcantieri now have two oil tankers of 80,000 tons each on their slips at Monfalcone and Sestri, and the Government is reorganising the whole industry so as to make it competitive in the fiercely competitive world of ship-building. Italcantieri and the Fiat company have recently formed a consortium, *la Società Grandi Motori*, which will establish works for building ships' engines at Trieste. The Italian merchant fleet now amounts to more than 6 million tons, and the Government is taking advantage of every opportunity which State power offers it to increase shipbuilding efficiency and production. About 400,000 tons of shipping were completed in 1966. A further 300,000 were launched, and keels were laid for 450,000 tons. Italy comes eighth among world shipbuilding countries.

MOTOR VEHICLES

As in Great Britain, the automobile industry has become the most prominent branch of the engineering industry and the index, if not also the mainstay, of production in most other fields. The names of the biggest Italian makers are well known : Fiat *(Fabbrica Italiana Automobili Torino)* of Turin, the biggest car factory in Europe and the support of the whole city, Lancia (also Turin), Alfa Romeo (Milan), Maserati (Modena), Ferrari (Brescia), and Lamborghini.

Production of motor vehicles of all kinds amounted to 1,300,000 units in 1966. Motor scooters and bicycles numbered 600,917. Production of tractors amounted to 67,717 units. The home market is still far from saturated; as mentioned before, the average of car ownership is one car to every two families, and families buy new cars relatively frequently. There is also a large and increasing export market. Exports of motor vehicles between January and October 1966 were 22 per cent above the figure for the corresponding period in 1965 (330,266 exported in 1966, 277,715 in 1965). In 1965, 18,947 tractors were exported; 22,432 in 1966.

The following are figures for manufacture of motor *cars* in Italy in 1966 :

		per cent of total
Fiat	1,110,701	86.7
Alfa Romeo	59,971	4.7
Autobianchi (Fiat)	37,427	2.9
Lancia	36,988	2.9
Innocenti	35,967	2.8
	1,281,054	100.0

Italy came fourth amongst Western European car manufacturing countries for numbers of vehicles in 1966, after Britain (1,413,146 produced by four main firms), France (1,780,533 by four main firms), Germany (2,524,693 by four main firms). The 35,967 cars attributed to Innocenti in the list above refer to the Morris cars manufactured in Italy under licence (Mini Minor, Morris 1100).

The general increase in production of motor vehicles in 1966, amounting to no less than 16.1 per cent in respect of the previous year, may be contrasted with the figure of 1.1 per cent for all countries with a market economy. The Italian firms are in fierce competition amongst themselves. The strongest opposition to Fiat comes from Alfa Romeo, of Varese, a subsidiary of the IRI and best known for its range of luxury and speed cars. In 1950 this company produced only 323 vehicles at its Portello factory. In 1967 production will amount to 70,000 vehicles, and will soon rise to 100,000. This is so far not much in comparison with the total of 1,384,000 vehicles produced by Fiat in the single year 1966, but the Alfa Romeo company is going on to build a factory at Naples which will produce 300,000 cars a year.

AIRCRAFT

The aircraft industry is also very active. Eighteen new aircraft from Italian makers were exhibited at the International Exposition at Le Bourget in May 1967. Four of these were of special interest : the G-91/Y light subsonic fighter, already mentioned in connection with the Air Force, a light three-seater single-engine plane known as the AM3 and owing something to the well known German Stork aircraft of the last war, a four-seater touring plane, Siai S 208 (with a piston engine) and the MB326 G, a more powerful and armed version of a well known Italian training craft which has already had much success. Other aircraft produced by Italy in recent years and exhibited at Le Bourget included the supersonic fighter F-104/G, now out of production, a light transport, one-engine plane, the AL-60, and two light touring planes.

Besides Fiat the most outstanding aircraft manufacturer in Italy at present is the Agusta company of Milan, which makes helicopters, partly from its own designs and partly under licence from the United States Bell Company. Its latest model is a large three-turbine helicopter, the Agusta 101/G. The Agusta company's helicopters make Italy the second world exporter of this type of craft. The Siai Company mainly makes tourist and other light aircraft. This sector of Italian industry is a curiously neglected one, and it receives little financial aid from the State. It has to face fierce competition from the British and French industries, and is obliged to work from foreign licences. There is no production of large passenger aircraft, and so Italian airlines (Alitalia) use British, French and United States makes.

OTHER HEAVY ENGINEERING

Other branches of heavy engineering in which Italy has always excelled, and with which she is now penetrating foreign markets, are construction of steel tubing for general purposes and large-scale enterprises, such as hydro-electric works. The main factories are at Brescia and Taranto. The tooling industry employs 25,000 persons and annual production takes third place after that of West Germany and Britain. There is a big factory at San Bernardo d'Ivrea, and a large boring mill is situated at Brescia. Another rapidly-developing branch is that of plant and apparatus for lifting, and cranes in general; the main centre of production is at Arluno, Milan. Submarine cables are made at

Pozzuoli, Naples. The thermal shields of the Europa I vector rocket launched at Woomera, Australia, were made in Italy.

LIGHT ENGINEERING

But perhaps Italians are at their best in the light engineering industry, which gives more scope and outlet to their designing abilities and craftsmanship, needs less raw materials and is more adapted to the use of electrical energy. There has been remarkable expansion in this field since the war, and perhaps the production of light motor bicycles and scooters should be noticed in this regard rather than in connection with heavy industry, for the Lambretta and other scooters were directly developed out of the small-tubes industry. Motor-cycles are made at Milan (the Bianchi company) and Moto Guzzi has its factories at Mandello-Lario near Como; the Olivetti typewriter company has its headquarters at Ivrea; optical and scientific instruments are made mainly at Turin and Florence; ball-bearings and adding machines at Villar Perosa, near Pinerolo in Piedmont. The Vespa motor-scooter is made at Lambrate and the Lambretta at Pontedra in Lombardy. Sewing machines are manufactured at Milan and Pavia (the Necchi company).

Italy comes third after the United States and West Germany in world production of typewriters. There are about 200 factories for making cooking stoves and food-heating appliances, but only about fourteen of these are operating on an industrial scale. They satisfy domestic demand and about 50 per cent of production is sold to foreign markets. There is a big washing-machine factory at Brugherio, Milan, and many other kinds of light engineering products are made all over the country. In 1966 production of sewing machines amounted to 650,372; standard typewriters 273,366; portable typewriters 491,170; calculating machines 602,790; roller ballbearings 101,981,000; electric lamp bulbs 436,542,000; lighting tubes (by elements) 888,624.

ELECTRONICS

Automatic engineering and electronics is a field in which Italy falls behind other Western countries. Olivetti developed the Gamma computer and began to develop another one, known as the Elea. But the company underwent an administrative and ownership crisis and the computers division of the firm was merged with General Electric. IBM and Remington also make United States machines in Italy, but Italian industry feels that it needs to invent and develop its own electronics side, since electronics is one of the keys to all general development. It is feared that unless this activity is taken out of United States hands, put back under Italian control and entrusted to Italian brains, Italy will be in danger of suffering a new period of colonialism and underdevelopment. This is a problem to which the Government, the IRI and the Higher Council for Scientific Research are giving serious attention. There is a large market for all kinds of electronic computers and similar machines, and the civil service is to be equipped with many.

THE CHEMICAL INDUSTRY

Lack of coal impeded early production of those chemicals which are normally got from coking and the full cycle of iron and steel production; Italy has no deposits of rock salt, in which Britain abounded, and potash, in which Germany and France had advantages. Italy's advantages came from her possession of hydro-electric power, sulphur, and a variety of small deposits of borax, gypsum, pyrites, fluorite and steatite. In 1939 the range of chemical products covered only ten main items. In 1966 it included thirty. Once more, the disasters of the war called forth a big effort in this industry, and there is now a large export trade in chemical products. The discovery of methane and oil in the subsoil was the largest single factor in this general advance. The annual increase in production (5.1 per cent) is higher than the annual increase for Italian industry as a whole (about 4.1 per cent). At the beginning of 1966 the industry employed 406,000 persons (170,000 in 1958). The chief centres of the chemical industry are in the north, over a wide area, at Portiglione in Tuscany and Empedocle and Gela in Sicily, all these producing phosphate fertilisers.

This industry is notable for the great amounts of capital and research that it requires. For this reason, and also because of the prime importance of petroleum products in the development of chemicals, it was largely brought under the control of the Montecatini group and the ENI. In 1965 the ENI invested £7½ million in petrochemicals, and work is continually going on at integrating production cycles, improving plant performance and reducing running costs. The large ammonia plant at Gela is being doubled in size; large advances are being made in the production of urea, ethylene, poly-ethylene and complex fertilisers. Plants for reforming methane are being built at the ports where storage vessels offload frozen methane into the pipelines. The factory at Ravenna for ammonia synthesis is being enlarged and a new factory is being built for making nitric acid. In connection with the plans for the industrialisation of the south, the ENI has established plants in the Basento valley in Calabria, for polymerisation of caprolactam and for making acrylic fibres.

Perhaps the most notable development has been that situated at Ravenna. This famous city remained a small coastal town until only ten years ago. Through the discovery of methane in the vicinity, it has suddenly become the great centre of the petrochemical industry, and a new port has been opened up with inland communications by canal and river as far as Milan. Chemical factories were established near the sources of methane for producing fertilisers, resins and, above all, synthetic rubber.

RUBBER

The Italian rubber industry began in 1872, when Pirelli opened his first factory at Milan, which remained the only one in the country for the following twenty years. By 1929 Italy was the fourth largest world exporter of rubber products, particu-

larly motor tyres. The exigencies of the second world war led to
the development of synthetic rubber; after several serious crises
the industry came to consist of about a hundred active firms by
1950, with Pirelli well in the lead. The industry expanded together with the automobile industry, and synthetic rubber came
to make up 44 per cent of all production. The rubber industry was the first to recover from the crisis that preceded the
economic boom of 1964, and by 1966 production amounted to
double that of 1959. The main items are tyres, adhesives, ebonite,
soles, heels, piping, technical articles, footwear, aircraft tyres,
conveyor and driving belts, carpets and coverings, toys, sports
articles, foam rubber, hygienic and sanitary articles. The tyres
branch is the most important and provides the index to the
health of the whole industry. In 1966, when general production
was up 8.8 per cent on the previous years, production of car
tyres rose by 12.4 per cent.

TEXTILES

Italy has been celebrated for its textiles for many centuries,
ever since Florence, Milan, and many other smaller cities developed the industry and spread its wares over Europe in the early
Middle Ages. Mass production, with electric power and relatively cheap labour, did not begin until the present century. Unlike the other branches of industry, textiles is not a basic one,
providing materials and equipment to others, and, since the prosperity of those other branches has been fundamentally the result
of the necessity to re-equip a whole country, it has not shared
to a similar degree in their successes. In this it has resembled the
British textiles industry, which has suffered many crises since
the war and has had to be reorganised and cut back.

The reasons for this situation were that Italy was dependent
on imports for most raw materials, except hemp and silk, had a
low home consumption per head (less than half that of Great
Britain), and had to export 40 per cent of her cotton and
25 per cent of her woollen goods in order to keep in full
production. There was fierce foreign competition and factories

were relatively small. The industry concentrated on producing high-quality cloths and clothing with new and very appealing styles, with great success, and also went in for extensive development of artificial fibres, which can be made from methane and petroleum by-products and cellulose; the need to import raw materials was therefore reduced. In fact Italy was a pioneer in rayon before the war. Since the general economic recovery and advance that began in 1964, this industry has progressed rapidly, benefiting from the increasing demand and the expansion of the synthetic and artificial fibre industry.

COTTON

The cotton industry is chiefly concentrated around Milan (Gallarate, Busto Arsizio and Legnano), but there are smaller centres at Pisa, Prato, Naples, and in Calabria. Most cotton is imported from the United States and India. The industry employs about 300,000 persons, and in 1965 produced 201,000 tons of yarn and 146,000 tons of cloth, including rayon cloth. These figures showed a decline of about 12.5 per cent on the previous year.

ARTIFICIAL FIBRES

By contrast production of artificial and synthetic fibres and cloth has been rising. About 70 per cent of the cellulose needed is produced in Italy, and efforts to increase supplies are being made by planting forests of eucalyptus in the south. The factories are large and are situated in Turin, at Varedo in Lombardy, and in the Basento valley in Calabria. In 1966 production of cellulose fibres was 185,000 tons; production of non-cellulose fibres amounted to 143,000 tons.

WOOL

The woollen industry is also very much dependent on imports, even though Italy has from ten to twelve million sheep. The main centres are Biella in Piedmont and Prato in Tuscany; there are many smaller mills in the valleys of the subalpine hills between Bergamo and Vicenza, where waterfalls abound. The industry's economic situation is very similar to that of the other branches of the textiles industry; that is to say it is undergoing a slight depression.

ARTISANS AND CRAFTSMEN

Arts and crafts flourish widely in Italy, and demand for their products is increasing. Their shops and booths are a feature in all parts, especially the older parts, of town and cities. They are progressively modernising their equipment and equipping themselves to fight the Goliath of modern industrial production. Some of the best known centres are the Venetian lagoon towns (glass and pottery), Faenza in Romagna (pottery-faience), Orvieto, Deruta and Assisi in Umbria, Vietri near Amalfi, Pescara and Castelli in the Abruzzi, Ruvo and Grottaglie in Apulia (all pottery), Burano (in the Venetian lagoon, lacemaking), Florence and Venice (gold and silver filigree and fine glass). Fine marble work is done at Carrara and Pietrasanta in Tuscany; Volterra, also in Tuscany, is known for its alabaster work, Siena for its onyx. Certain valleys in South Tyrol are celebrated for their woodcarving. Straw-working (hats, bags, baskets) flourishes at Florence and in Sardinia, and in Rome itself the old streets bearing the names of crafts still contain them—for example, Via dei Sediari has basket and chair weavers; for nuts and bolts, locks and keys you may go to Via dei Chiavari, and for household scales to the street next to it; for your clothes to Via dei Giubbonari, and so on.

The women's fashion industry has had success since the war. It is mainly centred on Florence. The Government intends to aid and encourage artisans and craftsmen in every way. They have an insurance system of their own, and State contributions to this fund may soon rise to 60 per cent of the whole.

FINANCE

The main material factors in the current Italian industrial and social revolution are the existence of a large number of previously unemployed, underemployed and poor people, and of abundant capital, wisely administered. It is well known that the present phase of boom conditions, 'the economic miracle', results from vast loans obtained from the United States in 1964 to give new life to depressed industries, to support the falling lira and to avert a grave political change. Finance is the key to the whole situation, and it is organised very differently in Italy than in Great Britain. On the one hand Italian banks are much more numerous, on the other hand the State has controlling holdings in both industry and banking through the IRI (Industrial Reconstruction Institute).

The IRI acquired its position in banking through its measures to overcome the great economic crisis of the early 1930s. Banks which had been merchant and investment banks were obliged to become deposit banks only, and special credit institutions were separately set up to provide capital for commerce and industry. Some of these institutions were formed by the deposit banks themselves. The law of 1936 which made these arrangements is still in force; its main purpose is to keep the banks solvent and to ensure that their operations are in accordance with the national interest. The Bank of Italy *(Banca d'Italia)* broadly performs the same functions as the Bank of England in Britain.

The clear distinction in Italy between short-term commercial credit and medium and long-term credit for large-scale and public enterprises is heightened by specialisation. Six banks are known as 'Institutes in Public Law' (chartered banks): the Bank of Naples, Bank of Sicily, Banca Nazionale del Lavoro, Istituto di San Paolo di Torino, Monte de' Paschi di Siena, and the Bank of Sardinia. These, together with the Banca Commerciale Italiana (headquarters in Milan), the Credito Italiano (Genoa) and the Bank of Rome, are the main suppliers of short-term commercial, agricultural and private credit. But there are also 156 other large banking institutions, 213 co-operative banks,

38 private banks and other credit institutes. The large banks mentioned operate savings accounts besides the usual other accounts, and there are also 79 savings banks, 731 rural and workers' banks, various Monti di Pietà and other similar credit and pledge banks, a feature of Italian life, dating back to the Middle Ages : the banks give credit against pledges of even quite modest personal belongings—the operation known in Britain as pawnbroking. Several Italian banks were founded in the Middle Ages.

The banks which operate as private banks but are owned by the IRI are known as ' Banks of National Interest '. They are the Banca Nazionale del Lavoro, the Banca Commerciale Italiana, Credito Italiano, and the Bank of Rome. Their main task is to provide medium-term loans to industry and agriculture, and they do this through their credit institute, the Mediobanca, against security provided by shares, raw materials and manufactured goods. Other such credit institutes are the Consortium for Loans against Industrial Shares, and the Istituto Mobiliare Italiano, which grants long-term funds to industry and shipping and provides counterpart funds for operations arising from dollar loans. The Ente Finanziamenti Industriali is a private bank supplying medium and long-term credit to certain kinds of industry. The banks having most overseas operations and branches are the Banca Nazionale del Lavoro, the Banca d'America e d'Italia, the Banca Commerciale Italiana, and Credito Italiano, all of which do much business with Britain.

There has been such a hunger for capital in Italian industry that the credit arrangements just described were found to be inadequate, and firms unable to be satisfied by the specialised credit institutes raised capital by short-term borrowing from private banks. This resulted in an inflationary situation which led to the crisis of 1964, solved in the end by importing vast new supplies of capital from the United States. The fact that industrial firms could turn to the private banks, in spite of the State policy which forbids that course, shows that industry is far from being as subject to State control as the existence of the IRI and its subsidiaries may suggest.

The year 1966 was a good year for Italian industry and the economy generally. According to the Governor of the Bank of Italy, Guido Carli, the measures necessary for maintaining success and getting rid of some negative elements include the greatest possible investment in renewal of plant and progress in technology, for which firms will need high profits. Wages and salaries should be regulated in view of the prime need to plough profits back into industry; credit institutions ought to be liberal in their loans to industry, and certain fiscal reforms ought to be introduced in order to encourage firms to invest in their own futures and to encourage investors to make their contributions without fear. Public spending, the greatest single inflationary factor and danger to the economy, should be reduced and also be aimed at correcting imbalances occurring in the economy from the activities of private enterprise. Production costs must be lowered, and one way to do this is by merging small firms into bigger ones and concentrating industries regionally according to their specialisation, rather than dispersing the same industry over the whole country.

These recommendations do not fit in entirely with the Government's programme, which takes political and social, not only economic factors, into account. The Government's main considerations are the need to provide certain essential public services with capital, to attain substantial equality of income between industry and agriculture, and to raise the level of life in the south up to that of the rest of the country. It is devoting large sums to development of middling and small industries all over the country, so as to counteract the harmful social effects of monopoly and large-scale concentration. This policy is to be applied to the greatest possible extent in the south and the islands.

There are stock exchanges at Turin, Milan, Genoa, Naples and Rome. There are 40,500 *società per azioni*, joint-stock companies which issue shares. About half the shares on the market are held by banks and credit institutes; about 40 per cent are held directly by the State and the rest are in the hands of about 225,000 shareholders. In other words, only 15 out of every

1,000 Italian families hold stock. This is a very low proportion in comparison with other Western countries, and one of the points in the Government's programme is to stimulate private investment and encourage firms to look for capital from private sources. Private credit for personal use is far harder to obtain from banks in Italy than it is in Britain, and consequently there are numerous institutes which specialise in this field.

AGRICULTURE

Italy has always been trying to increase the area of her cultivable terrain, which is limited by the fact that the most accessible land has been worked for three thousand years and that most of the country is mountainous or hilly. There are about 760 million acres of land in the whole country; 22 per cent of this area consists of plains, 38 per cent is mountains and 40 per cent hills. The increases and improvements dating from all ages, and visible on all sides, are due above all to the hard work and tenacity of many generations of peasants, and in modern times to land reclamation, improved methods of cultivation and, finally, mechanisation.

The first general census of Italian agriculture ever made, in

———

Young Italy: the elementary school at Coroglio in the province of Como. Italian children wear smocks to school (which boys change for jackets at a certain age).

1961, showed that there were 4.3 million holdings or farms on an area of more than 500 million acres and the majority (three-quarters) were being farmed directly by their occupiers. In 1951 the working agricultural population amounted to about 8,000,000, 42 per cent of the total labour force of the country. In July 1966 it amounted to only 4,700,000 persons, about 25 per cent of the whole working population; in Britain only 2 per cent of the working population is employed in agriculture and fisheries combined.

The most notable recent developments have been agrarian reform and closer settlement, greater use of mechanisation and fertilisers, and advances in irrigation. The area under irrigation has been doubled since 1961 and about $2\frac{1}{4}$ million tons of fertilisers were used in 1966. There are now more than 1,150,000 agricultural machines and motors in use; the number of tractors (500,000) represents an increase of 1,000 per cent over the last ten years. A factor limiting outright, large-scale mechanisation is the social policy which keeps farms small and numerous (there are no less than 1,421,000 very small holdings, 30 per cent of the total, which are no larger than $2\frac{1}{2}$ acres and have an average size of $1\frac{1}{4}$ acres). Mechanisation does not become feasible until the farm covers from 25 to 75 acres, according to

———

The beginning of the academic year at the University of Parma, founded in 1502. Italy has about fifty universities, spread all over the country. Most date from the Middle Ages, and in our day there has been little need to found new ones. Instead the old universities are being expanded.

the locality and quality of the soil. Peasants are therefore forming machinery co-operatives and also integrating holdings to some extent. A law of 1952 provided financial aids to peasants for the purchase of agricultural machinery and irrigation works and for constructing farm buildings, and by 1960 about 120,000 farm machines had been bought in this way. The regions with most machines on farms are Emilia-Romagna, the Veneto, Piedmont and Lombardy, which together possess about half the total. The average annual working rate of a tractor is from 600 to 800 hours, and its average life is from 10 to 12 years at that rate. Mechanisation of this kind is bringing about important changes in the farmer's relationship with and attitude towards the land and work; it is also altering the appearance of the countryside.

AGRARIAN REFORM AND LAND RECLAMATION

The recent agrarian reconstruction in Italy has been described as the most admirable piece of social reform carried out in Europe since the war. For about a century before that the peasantry of northern and central Italy had been acquiring more or less control over the land it worked, either through obtaining ownership or by means of the *mezzadria*—share-farming—system, in which the landlord provides the land, capital and improvements and the tenant pays him up to 50 per cent of the crop. This system prevails in northern and central Italy in places where the land is not already owned by the peasants. The *mezzadria* system is often criticised, but it has advantages for both sides and has survived social changes.

In the south things were rather different. Ever since the end of the Punic Wars and the time of the Gracchi the south had been agriculturally depressed. The ancient Roman government turned it into enormous latifundia for grazing and large-scale wheat production. It largely kept this character until very recent times. The peasantry did not own the land, and feudalism lived on into the twentieth century.

The Agrarian Reform Acts passed in 1950 were based on the principle that the land should be in the hands of those who work it. Large areas of the great southern estates were badly neglected by their owners; those parts that were being well farmed were left with landlords (within certain limits), and the rest was made over to the peasants; the landlords were compensated with Treasury bonds. The area expropriated was equivalent to about 4 per cent of the whole area of Italy, and 70 per cent of it was in the south; the rest was mainly in Tuscany (the Maremma), Sardinia and the Po delta. About 120,000 families received land. The new farms varied in size from $6\frac{3}{4}$ to $47\frac{1}{2}$ acres according to the region and type of farming. The average size of farms, as distinct from allotments, was $22\frac{1}{2}$ acres. The reform agencies made everything ready for the new owners, who were given houses on their farms rather than away from them in villages, as has been usual. The reformers had mainly social and political aims in view, but there have been objections to economic aspects of their work, especially as regards the size of farms. The inherited outlook of the southern peasant has also been a hindrance to full success; he is averse to entering co-operatives, and unaccustomed to taking initiatives.

Land reclamation goes together with agrarian reform. The Romans reclaimed most of the swampy and forest lands of the Po valley before the Christian era; when those lands became degraded during the Gothic and Lombard periods, Cistercian monks reclaimed them again. This story is typical of what happened all over Italy, and, indeed, Europe. Much reclamation has gone on in modern times, most notably in the Maremma heathlands north of Rome and the Pontine marshes to the south of the city. Two and a quarter million acres have been reclaimed since 1938.

In recent years there has been increasing movement off the land to the towns. One reason for this is that the agricultural worker's real income amounts to only about half the real income of a worker in industry. There is a danger that agricultural production will decline, paradoxically just when there is greater home demand for it than ever before owing to the greater spending power of the cities. The Government is therefore making every possible effort to bring about a balance between town and country in incomes and living conditions. The main measures will be commercialisation of agricultural produce, that is to say, emphasis will be laid on cash crops, especially vegetables, fruit and animal products, and on mechanisation and redistribution of land for intensive and extensive farming respectively. The output of the individual land worker will be raised, together with the general productivity of the soil (about £123 million will be spent on soil and general land improvement). The Ministry of Agriculture is going to set up local agricultural boards *(enti)* with the task of carrying the general reconstruction through.

AGRICULTURAL PRODUCE

In spite of its mountains and hills, Italy has a higher proportion of arable land than all European countries except Poland and Denmark. But high yields from good soils are not so extensive; also, rain is rare and unreliable in much of the south and the islands.

Cereals. Wheat is the main cereal crop, and Italy is second only to France in Europe as a wheat producer. The country became an importer of wheat during the last decades of the last century, and the resulting drain on foreign reserves led the State to introduce a new system of protection in 1936. Imports were made a government monopoly, and a compulsory pooling system was set up for all home-grown wheat. The Government fixed the price to the farmer every year, and also the price at which home and imported wheat was sold to the mills. This arrangement gradually led to a reversal in the national wheat balance from a deficit to a surplus position. The present situation is that domestic yields have greatly increased in the last six years and imports have therefore been reduced. The grain most in demand is hard wheat for pasta. Quality of grain is also being improved. The greatest areas under wheat are in the south, but the highest yields are in the north and centre. Rice is another staple article of diet, grown around Vercelli and Novara in Piedmont and Lomellina in Lombardy. The country is self-sufficient in this grain and has good prospects of outlets in the Common Market.

Vines. The vine is a major plant in very many regions, and an average of 10 to 11 million tons of grapes are harvested every season. All but about 7 per cent are used for wine (6½ to 7 million tons of wine). The main northern vine-growing areas are Piedmont, Veneto, the Trentino and Friuli. Tuscany is famous for its Chianti and other wines; Latium produces about 22 million gallons a year, and the chief southern regions are Apulia (high alcohol content) and Campania; Sicily and Sardinia also produce great quantities. Italy supplies the world with a quarter of all its wine. Present policy in this sector is to reduce production and to improve quality and standards. Since the war co-operative efforts have been made to give production of the classic wines of Italy the kind of cachet enjoyed by French wines. One organisation guarantees the authenticity and quality of the wines produced by its members. The Government has introduced stringent laws to suppress the once all too common practices of adulteration and falsification (the generic Italian term for which is *sofisticazione*). The Carabinieri have a special branch which administers these laws; it has brought some astounding frauds to light. Penalties are very severe.

Olives. Italy comes second only to Spain as a producer of olives. Production amounts to 2¼ million tons of olives and nearly half a million tons of oil a year. Apulia is the greatest single producing region, and is followed by Calabria, Sicily and Tuscany, where quality is best. More and more trees are being planted every year, and so great is the demand for oil that importations have to be made from Spain. But in 1965 Italian production exceeded that of Spain for the second time.

Vegetables. Town and country are closely linked, and every city and town has many street vegetable and fish markets, besides general markets and covered markets in some quarters. The markets chiefly sell the produce of the surrounding countryside (sheep still graze and vegetables still grow by the very walls of Rome). The Campania, volcanic hinterland of Naples, is far in the lead in this field, and has the most varied crops. It supplies Naples and Rome and also grows early and spring vegetables for foreign markets in central and northern Europe. The range of vegetables is very wide, and beside the characteristically Italian vegetables—artichokes, aniseed and various kinds of beans—there are many tropical and sub-tropical fruits and vegetables such as the eggplant and courgette. There is also a flourishing canning, jam and marmalade industry. Tomato sauce for pasta and preserved tomatoes are mainly made at Nocera, near Naples.

Fruit. This branch of agriculture, which of course has a very long history in Italy, began to assume large-scale and intensive proportions at the beginning of this century, in the Trentino and South Tyrol at first, then in Lombardy, Emilia-Romagna and finally in Apulia, Abruzzi and Sicily. The main fruits are apples, pears, cherries, peaches, apricots, citrus, almonds, walnuts, grown in a specialised way according to climatic regions. There is now a very large export of all kinds of fruits, centred mainly around Verona for apples, pears, peaches and apricots, and Naples, Bari and Palermo for the rest. Peaches, so rare and unripe in England, abound in Italy.

Preservation of fruit by deep freezing did not begin in Italy until after the war. Today there are 686 fruit-freezing plants, 633 of which are in the north. Gas storage is being developed. Fruit growing is done largely on a co-operative basis. The south specialises in almonds, apricots and dried fruits, but production of dried fruits has sharply declined in recent years. Production of hazel nuts, however, has gone up. Chestnuts abound, and are sold roasted in the streets of cities throughout the winter.

Sicily is the biggest producer of citrus fruits, and in recent years has grown 50 per cent of all oranges, 62 per cent of all tangerines and mandarins, and 90 per cent of the lemon crop. Exports go to the five continents. Until means were found of preserving and marketing fresh fruit in the north, most exports came from the south and the islands. Italian agriculture and fruitgrowing have the obvious advantage over most of the rest of Europe of seasons coming in earlier.

Floriculture. This is a major activity in Liguria and indeed in all Italy. The Ligurian flowerbeds have doubled in area since 1951. Carnations, roses, tuberoses, gladioli and chrysanthemums are mainly exported, but there is also a large home demand.

Fodder crops. Fodder crops are grown on 25,000,000 acres and production amounts to 40 to 42 million tons a year. Milk and beef cattle are usually kept to the stall. Animal husbandry is practised widely over the area where most fodder is grown, that is to say, the north and centre, where livestock are raised by intensive means. Lombardy, Emilia and Tuscany are best known for this activity, but the mountainous areas in the north produce high quality milk, butter and cream, and dairying has become very intensive around the big cities. The case of Rome is a good example. The Roman Campagna was once a vast dry heath, grazed by sheep and goats; now it is covered with market gardens and dairy farms.

FISHERIES

The seas of Italy are not rich in fish. Fishing on the west coast is only local, and the seas on the east coast are very deep, with a very narrow continental shelf. Nevertheless, quite large fleets of trawlers put out from Ancona, Pescara, Bari and smaller ports on the east, and Genoa, Leghorn, Naples and Reggio on the west coast. The main Sicilian fishing ports are Syracuse, Trapani, Ragusa and Palermo. Fleets go as far as the Moroccan coasts and the Newfoundland Banks. The Sicilian fleets work along the coasts of North Africa. The main fish landed are anchovy, sardine and mackerel. Tunny fishing is carried on in season off the coasts of Sicily. Large quantities of shellfish and crustaceans are also landed. The Adriatic waters provide about half the total of all fish landed, the Tyrrhenian a fifth.

FORESTS

The forests of Italy suffered badly during the centuries. The State has been making efforts for many years to repair the damage and degradation. Remnants of the ancient forests remain in remote areas and on highlands where rainfall is more abundant, and especially on volcanic soils on the Sila and Aspromonte high plains in the far south and in the Apennines of the centre; conifer forests are quite extensive in the alpine highlands of the north. The Fascist régime encouraged some deforestation during its drive to increase agricultural production. Re-afforestation is now the rule. The State Forest Service, employs 7,000 men, and has 18 regional inspectorates, 74 departments, 33 districts, and 1,600 forest stations. Italy has always had to import timber, but re-afforestation is reducing that need.

THE SOUTHERN DEVELOPMENT FUND

The *Cassa del Mezzogiorno* (Southern Development Fund), was set up in 1951, under a Minister for Southern Development, with the task of raising the south's economy nearer the level of that of the north, so as to give the whole peninsula a balanced life (but there are some who argue that the general trend should be accepted, and that the south should be developed as a solely agricultural domain, feeding the industrial north). The main instrument of the Fund is the Industrial Reconstruction Institute—IRI; its activities have now extended somewhat north of the ' border ' and its general scope has continued to widen. Its main tasks were to improve agriculture, to set up an industrial infrastructure and improve environmental conditions. It is generally agreed that the Fund has done very good work, yet there is still much disagreement about what it ought to have done and what it ought to be doing now. It is also generally agreed that after sixteen years results have not lived up to hopes.

SHOPS

The most salient feature of Italian domestic trade and shopkeeping in general is that it is a matter of small family businesses. Chain stores, monster department stores, combines and great chains of shops selling standardised goods at fixed prices are conspicuously absent by comparison with Great Britain, though there are two chains of modest size, Cim and Standa. The same goes for supermarkets, though this kind of trade finds some favourable soil among the new industrial masses around some of the northern cities, but in general it is being effectively limited, if not altogether excluded from Italy. There are a number of small department stores, dating from the end of the last century, but these have developed very few of the characteristics of low-quality standardised mass commerce. The tendencies are all in favour of increased diversification and liberalisation of production and distribution, although the limited advantages of having some supermarkets are recognised and there is a willingness to meet the desires of the mass foreign tourist trade. Instead of letting small businesses be closed down or absorbed because of rising costs, the Government is actively encouraging them to solve their problems by co-operative methods.

In 1966 there were 760,000 retail shops and 400 supermarkets. The Italian feels happy buying in the square and street markets because he is buying fresh goods direct, on a human basis. The shopkeeper's activity is not only his way of making money but also his and his family's life; whereas the owner or tenant of the supermarket desires merely to make money from anyone who comes in, and the results are dehumanising. The same applies to every other kind of trading activity. There are no chains of standardised restaurants selling low-quality food at high prices.

There are about 210,000 bars in Italy, an average of one for every 210 inhabitants. There are no licensing hours, and the Government is at present introducing a law which will make licensing of public premises and shops even more liberal than it is at present. Shop hours are extremely comprehensive, being generally from eight in the morning to half-past one and from five to seven-thirty or eight in the evening. The Italian housewife goes to the markets and shops early in the morning, and does her evening shopping between six and eight. Until recently food shops were always open on Sunday mornings; now they are closed, but are still open on holiday mornings. On the eve of holidays they stay open one or two hours later than usual. Shopping hours are fixed at the beginning of each season of the year by the praetor of the city or province, whose concern is for the public interest and convenience.

Salt and tobacco are government monopolies. One buys one's salt in the tobacco shop, which also sells a large variety of other small necessities, including stamps. Certain members of parliament recently introduced a bill to close tobacco shops on Sundays, but the bill has been amended to require a certain proportion to remain open in turn, for the convenience of the public. There are many all-night chemists' shops and pharmacies, which also have a rotary system of remaining open on Sundays.

Retail trade organisations are seeking sources of credit to lay a co-operative basis to their wholesale buying and to obtain tax reliefs, especially in the turnover tax. The number of people employed in the trade has risen in recent years by about 45,000 to 2,500,000.

In the years 1955-66 retail trade sales increased by figures ranging from 215 per cent to 1,637 per cent and 1,337 per cent (the last two figures refer to clothing and radio, television and music respectively).

It has been estimated that £980 million were spent on private consumption in Italy in 1965, and only 7 per cent of this was spent in big stores, especially supermarkets (the figure for Great Britain is 50 per cent, for the United States 90 per cent). In 1961 there were 589,000 industrial producers selling through 663,000 shops. The number of retail shops was 502,000 in 1951; today, as has been mentioned, it is 760,000.

The difference between the cost of production of an article and its retail price is smaller in Italy than in any other Common Market country. Costs of distribution are also lower (27.26 per cent of the selling price, but in France 38.92 per cent and in Germany 50.04 per cent). One of the main reasons for this advantageous position is the fact that retail selling is predominantly in the hands of small shopkeepers.

Grocers who are convicted of having defrauded their customers in any way or sold spoilt goods are punished with fines and by having their shops shut down for certain periods. The courts' sentences are also publicised.

FOREIGN TRADE

Until about 1960 Italy imported much more than she was able to export, but in more recent years there has been a marked change, and Italian firms have been steadily increasing their exports and extending their activities to countries that used to be closed or difficult to penetrate. Italy is also now exporting capital. The most significant single event in the history of her recent export trade is that it has become first and foremost orientated towards the Common Market, of which Italy is of course a foundation member. However, although exports continue to increase, in spite of temporary setbacks, at a more than satisfactory rate, imports have also increased and there is a slightly unfavourable balance of trade.

The main imports are fuel, raw materials, semi-finished materials, finished industrial goods, consumer goods, agricultural produce, foodstuffs and live animals.

Exports cover all goods and services. The sectors of industry which showed the greatest increases in exports in 1965 were metallurgy, engineering, petroleum derivatives, the chemical industry and clothing.

The main increases in exports of agricultural produce occurred in fruit and vegetables.

No other country has derived more advantages from membership of the Common Market, which has been one of the main factors in stimulating Italian industry and agriculture to achieve its great successes.

Exports to the Common Market have increased fivefold and imports from it have trebled, in comparison with the figures for 1957. Imports from other countries have more than doubled, and exports to them have increased two-and-a-half times. Exports to the United States increased by 21.9 per cent in 1965 compared with 1964. Exports to the Soviet Union increased by 20.8 per cent and those to China by 30.6 per cent. The Communist group of countries absorbs 5.4 per cent of Italian exports.

Trade with the other Common Market and European Free

Trade Association countries amounts in each case to only fractions of the trade done with West Germany and France. The next biggest European customer for Italy is Great Britain whose purchases are worth about a third of those of France and a quarter of those of West Germany. The advantage in trade with Italy is decisively with Britain. The main items of export from Britain to Italy are nonmetalliferous minerals, woollen cloth, iron and steel sheets, metals, non-electric engines, machines, motors and apparatus, with spare parts, precision engineering products, vehicle parts for assembly, pharmaceutics, and various products of the engineering and chemical industries. The main Italian exports to Britain are fresh fruit, tomato conserve, sauce and preserves, woollen cloths, leather footwear, non-electric engines, machines and spare parts, boats and spare parts, light and fuel oils, foodstuffs and wines. British tourists in Italy bring an invisible export of at least £50,000,000 a year; they numbered about a million in 1966.

The main Italian exports to all countries, but especially to those of the Common Market, consist of fresh fruit and vegetables, cotton, woollen, silk and artificial fibre cloths, leather footwear, rolled iron and steel, typewriters, office machines, telecommunications apparatus, motor cars, pharmaceutics, lubricating oils and marble. Its main articles of import from the Common Market countries are the same, with the addition of scrap metals, cheeses (from France), sugar, milk and butter. Italy lacks good cigars, except for the famous *toscano*, a taste for which definitely has to be acquired; cigars are imported from Germany, Belgium and South America. Trade with her other neighbours, Austria and Yugoslavia, is quite small in comparison, and the same may be said of trade with Spain and Greece and other Mediterranean countries. The balance of trade with Austria is steady, and Italy exports more industrial goods than she imports from Spain and Yugoslavia—agricultural imports mainly making up gaps in her own production of the same Mediterranean crops.

Italy has busy trade with all the countries of the British Commonwealth, above all with those which have large Italian communities. Figures show a rise of exports to all those countries except Ceylon, Singapore and Sierra Leone.

Another very large item in Italian overseas trade consists of Italian workers living in other lands. Italian industrial and engineering firms are very active all over the world, especially in the Middle East and Africa. The Hyde Park Corner underpass in London was built by an Italian firm, as was the Kariba Dam in Rhodesia. Sixteen major Italian industrial and engineering firms are at present carrying out projects in India, and a great number of smaller firms are also engaged in joint ventures there.

TRADE FAIRS

Numerous national and international trade fairs (92 in 1967) are held in Italy every year. The most important are at Turin, Milan, Rome, Naples and Bari.

SEAPORTS AND SHIPPING

The chief seaports are Genoa, La Spezia, Leghorn, Civitavecchia, Naples, Palermo, Syracuse, Taranto, Brindisi, Bari, Pescara, Ancona, Venice and Trieste. Genoa and Naples are by far the biggest and most important. They are rivals for trade with all the Americas and there are frequent sailings of large passenger liners for both the east and west coasts of the two continents. Naples and Genoa are main ports of call for British passenger ships bound for the East.

Genoa is the main seaport for Switzerland, which also owns ships based there. It is also important for trade between southern Germany and Austria and the Mediterranean, but is above all the main outlet for Milan, with which it is linked by good railways and motorways.

Palermo and Syracuse chiefly trade in fruit exports and with Africa. Taranto is one of the chief naval bases, and Brindisi and Bari between them share Italian trade with the Aegean and the Near East. Both these ports, and Pescara and Ancona, have sailings to Yugoslav ports. Venice no longer enjoys her old commanding position on the Adriatic, but she still enjoys a large volume of trade. Her place in the upper part of the Adriatic was taken during the nineteenth century by Trieste, developed by the Hapsburg monarchy as the natural outlet for southeastern Europe. After the end of the Austrian empire Trieste declined, but the Italian Government has taken measures to revive it by seeking agreements with Austria and other Danube countries and by establishing shipbuilding and related industries in the city. Genoa, Naples, Palermo, Taranto, Ancona, Venice and Trieste all have excellent natural harbours, but all these ports have also been endowed with first-rate artificial basins and facilities.

The main Italian shipping lines are the Finmare and the Flotta Lauro. The Finmare is a State corporation, formed in 1937. It is the holding company for the Italia, Lloyd Triestino and Adriatica lines, which have services to most ports in the world, with passenger services to the chief American, Eastern and Pacific ports. The flagships are the *Michelangelo* and the *Raffaello*, which came into service in 1965 and run to North America. The Flotta Lauro competes with the Finmare group with conspicuous success. There are local shipping services between the peninsula and the islands, around the Adriatic, to the Aegean and Levant, and Africa.

TRADES UNIONS AND EMPLOYERS' ORGANISATIONS

The industrial and social chaos which Mussolini had a hand in causing in the years before the first world war was aggravated after the war and brought the country to the edge of collapse. During his twenty years of power—*il Ventennio*—he suppressed the old Marxist and Catholic trades unions. His own system of labour organisations collapsed during the second world war. The Christian Democrats, Socialists and Communists reorganised their own trades unions, and founded the General Confederation of Labour (GCIL) in Rome in 1944.

The Christian Democrats soon broke away from the Communists and founded what eventually became known as the Italian Confederation of Workers' Unions—*Confederazione Italiana Sindacati Lavoratori,* with left-wing tendencies. Another group, of Social Democrats and Republicans formed the *Unione Italiana del Lavoro* (UIL), and, finally, right-wing workers set up the *Confederazione Italiana Sindacati Nazionali dei Lavoratori* (CISNAL). In spite of their political differences these organisations have usually maintained a united front where wage claims, working conditions and benefits are concerned. There is also the organisation called ACLI—*Azione Cattolica Lavoratori Italiani,* which has social and religious, not in the first place political aims.

The main agrarian organisation is the *Confederazione dei Coltivatori Diretti,* which represents the peasants and allotment holders. It is above all interested in obtaining social gains and benefits, and includes about half the agricultural working population.

On the employers' side the organisations are the *Confederazione Generale dell'Industria* (Confindustria), the *Confederazione Generale del Commercio* and the *Confederazione Generale dell'Agricultura.* All the general confederations have affiliated local and regional associations numbering several hundreds. Collective contracts are made between the two sides, and the Ministry of Labour is disposed to act as conciliator in disputes at the request of one or both parties.

In 1965 there were 3,191 labour conflicts involving strikes. The number of workers involved in strikes amounted to 2,309,800. Hours of work lost were 55,943,000. These figures may be compared with figures for strikes in Britain; an average of 20,000,000 hours a year.

WAGES

The following are some round figures of Italian rates of pay.

Industry	Average Monthly Pay
	£
Electricity, Gas and Water	90
Oil and Methane	80
Metallurgy	77
Printing	75
Chemicals	70
Manufacturing	50
Cotton, wool and synthetic fibres	50
Building	50

If the Italian figures seem low in comparison with some British rates of pay, it ought to be remembered that the cost of living is generally cheaper in Italy than in Britain and taxes are 20 per cent lower on the average. In addition there are a large number of payments by way of family allowances and overtime. Executives and managers in these same industries receive about double the pay of manual workers. A top manager in electricity will receive about three times as much as a manual worker.

———

A retractable gangway at Fiumicino airport, near Rome. Italy is in a central position for world air routes, and Alitalia, the State airline, maintains about ninety services to all parts of the world. Inland air services are also well run.

UNEMPLOYMENT

In round numbers, Italy had 1,117,000 unemployed employables in 1959; in 1966 she had 769,000. Comparatively speaking, Italy still has more unemployed than Holland, Sweden, Great Britain, Belgium and Austria, but less than Yugoslavia, Canada and the United States. Great Britain had about 500,000 unemployed in June 1967.

The Government hopes to be able to create 4,900,000 new jobs during the period 1965-80. Basic unemployment pay amounts to about £14 a month, with adjustments for spouse and children. This is roughly equivalent to the rates in force in Britain.

WOMEN AT WORK

In 1966 there were 5,289,000 women workers in Italy, out of a total female population of 21,361,000. Of these 5,078,000 actually had jobs for an appreciable period of time. Women thus make up about a quarter of the total working population.

Peasant women work with their husbands in the fields to greater and lesser degrees according to the season, and in 1966

Villagers on reclaimed land in the Maremma district of Tuscany (Ribolla, Grosseto), playing bowls. Note the poplar saplings and the new farmhouses.

H

the number of women so employed was 1,419,000. The number of women working in industry in the same period was 1,564,000, the vast majority in manufacturing industries. Those employed in other activities numbered 2,095,000, including 850,000 in commerce, 1,175,000 in banking, insurance, public administration and similar office jobs, and nursing etc.

As for office jobs and positions of command or responsibility held by women in working life, 420,000 women held such posts in agriculture in 1966. In industry 1,268,000 held them (1,242,000 in the manufacturing industries). The number given for other occupations is 1,429,000. The description of such posts refers to jobs such as that of a nurse, a forewoman in a factory, a cashier in an office, and so on. Besides all these figures, which refer to fully employed persons, there are many thousands of women who do part-time jobs in all fields. Numbers of women in employment are falling.

The social attitude towards employment of women is fairly clear. It is considered all right for peasant women to work, and for urban and town girls to work in factories, shops and offices. There is distaste for the idea of a ' career woman ', and girls working in shops and offices are usually paid on the assumption that they are living at home and have no one to keep. That is to say, they are paid less than men for the same jobs.

Official policy is that women should be given the opportunity to work in order to supplement the family income or to satisfy some talent, but that they should also be given every facility for being housewives and mothers at the same time. A law has recently established particular provisions for working peasant women, who will receive compensation payments of 12s. a day or £30 in a lump sum for absence from work, whether on their own or somebody else's land, through maternity.

SICKNESS AND INJURY BENEFITS

All Italian workers are insured against sickness and injury by the *Istituto Nazionale Infortuni sul Lavoro*—National Institute against Accidents at Work, INAIL, founded in the 1930s. This

Institute provides the same kinds of benefits as are provided by the National Insurance and Health schemes in Great Britain. As regards insurance as a whole, there are 166 public and privately-owned companies. Life insurance premiums amounted to 2.3 per cent of the national income in 1964, which is the lowest figure in Europe, apart from Portugal. The Government intends to encourage private life insurance by every means, while at the same time bringing social and health insurance under a national scheme.

Pensions for the old have already been mentioned. There are many kinds of invalid and war pensions, most of them quite small. The Government intends to raise them by about 25 per cent during the next few years, but the pensioners are pressing for a sliding scale of increases—*la scala mobile* or escalator system. Military pensions are probably at a higher rate than in Britain; a sergeant-major in the Air Force, after twenty-five years' service, is retired with a pension of about £95 a month.

POOR RELIEF

The basic civil means of relief to the needy is the *Ente Communale di Assistenza*, the Municipal Assistance Office, found in every commune. In the big towns and cities the ECA runs very cheap restaurants for the poor; they used to be much more numerous than they are now. Besides its traditional means of relief of the needy, the Church also has an organisation like the ECA, known as ONARMO.

5

How they Learn

SCHOOLS

EDUCATION is compulsory from the age of six to fourteen, the minimum period considered necessary for conscious participation in social affairs. In June 1967 the number of children at school amounted to 7,719,822. More than four million of these were in the elementary schools, and about two million in the intermediate and high schools. The rest were in all kinds of technical and professional training schools and institutions. There is strong emphasis on humanist studies. The choice between classical and scientific or technical studies is made at about the age of fifteen, after intermediate school *(scuola media)*. In 1959 14 per cent of the population was engaged in some form of study; in 1966 it was 15.9 per cent.

The Ministry of Education is now trying to provide all children with complete intermediate studies. At present about 90 per cent go from elementary to intermediate school, and 80 per cent of those go on to some form of higher studies, or training for industry, commerce, agriculture, the armed services or other avocations. Education begins at the age of four or five in the kindergarten, *scuola materna*. Primary school begins at five, and junior intermediate school at eleven. The new *scuola media unica* is a sort of comprehensive school, which gives three years' general education from eleven to fourteen or fifteen, when the choice between liberal and scientific or technical studies is made. There is also a *scuola di avviamento professionale* —professional training preparatory school; during the three years of each school it is possible to change from one to the other. Secondary or high school is known as the liceo *(Lycée-Lyceum)*. There are two kinds: *(liceo classico* and *liceo scientifico)*.

The *liceo classico* is based strongly on Latin and Greek and modern language studies. Philosophy is taught in the middle and high schools. Schooling is free in principle, but there are various supplementary and textbook charges. The primary schools are run by the communes and supported by the local taxpayers. Education is highly centralised in the Ministry, which draws up curriculums and to which reference must be made in all questions—there are various stories from earlier periods about the stringency of centralisation in Rome: an exasperated village schoolmaster sending a telegram to the Minister asking permission to allow a pupil to leave the room! Strict centralisation is a relic of the time when the Savoy monarchy was trying to create a unitary national culture. Education in each province is controlled by a Superintendent of Studies, or Director of Education *(Provveditore agli Studi)* appointed by the Ministry. There is no shortage of teachers, but there is a grave lack of schools and of desire for learning, especially in the south.

Figures published in June 1967 show that 117 out of every 1,000 schoolchildren obtain the higher certificate of education, *diploma*, at the end of the secondary school course. Children of entrepreneurs or businessmen and professional men represent 11.1 per cent; children of administrators, managers and office workers generally 38.3 per cent; children of dependent workers 21 per cent. Of the children who reach the last period of secondary education, 56.8 per cent have working class fathers.

School hours are different from those in England. Until problems of overcrowding arose, lessons were given only in the morning, and children were free for the rest of the day. Then two shifts were introduced, each class being divided into two, one for the morning, the other for the afternoon. Schools are now returning to the normal system of lessons in the morning only. In the kindergartens and elementary schools boys and girls

wear a blue or black smock with a broad white collar. In intermediate schools, or at least in some, boys discard the smock for
a jacket of the same material, worn over their clothes. Children
in high schools wear no uniforms.

Sports and games do not form a part of the ordinary school
curriculum. Italian schoolchildren become emancipated in many
ways earlier than English children, partly because they are not
confined to uniforms, such concepts as ' school spirit ' are not
nourished, and there is an absence of repressive discipline.
Lessons are also given in the form of lectures in the upper
classes, whereas in Britain this change does not usually occur
until university level. The Italian schoolchild is therefore expected to rely on his powers of attention and investigation
earlier.

The Catholic Church plays a great part in education. Most
children go to the State schools, but receive religious instruction
from priests who come in. Private schools have only a very small
proportion of all schoolchildren in Italy. Most of them are run
by Catholic religious orders. Many religious orders also run
public (not in the English sense) day schools, following State
curriculums and taking State examinations. There are very
many of these, and they are known as *scuole parificate*—equal-
ised schools. One important characteristic of schooling in Italy,
which is both a result and a cause of the social easiness which
Italy enjoys, is that there is very little class feeling in connection
with education. The school buildings in the cities are just like
other buildings around them, and all the eligible children from
the vicinity attend without much regard to their social class.
Young princes may sit side by side with waiters' sons. The
family does not try to shift its educational responsibility on to
schools; whatever is of value is known to come from family life,
the rest is only exterior knowledge. Hence few children are
sent away to boarding schools, which is regarded as a cruel
practice.

Schools providing for the upper classes certainly exist; for
example, the Istituto Massimo at Rome, a Jesuit school, founded
for the sons of the Roman aristocracy. Its scope is socially much

wider now. In many of the more important cities there are colleges run by foreign members of religious orders, and those who can afford it will send their children to these so that they may acquire foreign languages more easily. Rome is rich in such schools. Pope Pius XII's grand-nephews went to the Irish Christian Brothers' school there. There are two English schools in Rome for the children of British residents, and a number of ' international ' schools—i.e. American—schools, run by religious and secular institutions for the large foreign community in the City.

The census of 1961 showed that illiterates made up 8.4 per cent of the population. This figure is now estimated to have been reduced to about 6 per cent, since 600,000 illiterates have been given courses in reading and writing in the intervening years.

UNIVERSITIES

There are now 46 universities in Italy, in 29 cities. Some were founded in the Middle Ages: Bologna AD 1200, Naples 1224, Rome 1303, Turin 1404, Messina 1549. Later foundations were Urbino 1564, Cagliari 1626, Palermo 1805. More recent are Florence 1924, the University of the Sacred Heart, Milan 1920, Milan State University 1924, and Lecce 1959. Most universities were founded by the popes. Some are very big; Rome has 50,000 undergraduates. Others, such as Siena, with 1,000, are very small. The north contains 17 universities and colleges, with 86 faculties and 2 senior Institutes of Physical Education. Another 10 are situated in the centre, with 52 faculties and the Superior School at Pisa. There are 14 universities and university colleges in southern and insular Italy, with 62 faculties, and there are Higher Institutes of Physical Education in both the centre and south.

The oldest university in Italy, and Europe, was that of Salerno. It was celebrated for medicine, but no longer exists. Naples is renowned for its law studies, Bologna for medicine.

Students may move fairly freely around from university to university, beginning their course in one and finishing it in another. Examinations used to be fairly easy, but they have been made harder. Most are oral examinations. A liberal attitude, within certain limits, is taken towards failure; one may fail in February, take the examination again in June, then again in October if necessary, and so on, until one passes. The first degree is known as the *laurea*—the laurel wreath; the graduate is a *laureato*, and he is addressed as Doctor—*Dottore*. University examinations only give the privilege of the degree; in order to enter any profession, State examinations must also be taken.

There is no college system, such as obtains in some British universities. The university is usually one large building in the middle of the city, and students find quarters as best they may. There are *pensionati*, comparable to halls of residence. The terms are roughly similar to those in British universities. Undergraduates wear no such thing as a gown, but professors wear academic dress on ceremonial occasions. On festive occasions, such as carnival, students wear medieval hats, coloured according to the faculty.

The faculty system, with lectures, dominates in teaching. Some universities have only a few faculties. There are four grades of teachers: *assistente*, appointed, after examination, for a year; *libero docente*, a lecturer who receives a very small fee; *professore incaricato*, roughly equivalent to the Reader in a British university and appointed for annual periods at low pay; *professor titolare*, full professor, who obtains his post by competition and by having published some work. In the Italian language the word *professore* is a generic word for teacher. The strict term for professor in the British sense is *catedratico*—he who has the chair.

Teaching and courses are arranged in a rather impersonal way; for instance, at Rome, in the faculty of modern literature, students whose names begin with the first half of the letters of the alphabet read one set of authors and hear one professor, and the others read and hear another. On the other hand, whereas in Britain examinations are impersonal, in Italy they are very personal affairs, being oral for the most part, and results are made known immediately.

ACADEMIES AND INSTITUTES

A feature of Italian intellectual life is the number of academies, such as the Accademia di San Luca at Rome, founded in the fourteenth century, and the Accademia della Crusca at Florence, founded in 1582. There are twenty-six others in most of the historical cities, and they are concerned with arts and sciences. The Accademia di Santa Cecilia at Rome is a celebrated school of music. There are 36 foreign academies, schools and cultural missions. The British Council has a good library in Rome.

There are 63 Italian institutes for the arts and music, 57 higher institutes for scientific and social research, and 127 special research institutes, and also polytechnics, engineering, architecture and aerospace engineering schools, a National Institute for Higher Mathematics, and various institutes for African, Middle Eastern and Oriental Studies.

Except for the old academies, the Catholic universities, and the two independent universities of Urbino and Lecce, the Italian institutions are under strict Ministerial control, especially the universities, the rectors of which are appointed by the State. The rectors are now making moves to obtain more independence for themselves and their universities.

GRANTS

University education is not as financially free to the undergraduate as it is in Britain, but the State makes grants according to merit, for distribution by the universities themselves. About ten thousand new teachers are to be appointed to the universities in coming years, to meet the demands caused by an inflow of undergraduates benefiting from the new rules of financial assistance.

There is a university for foreigners at Perugia. Foreigners may freely attend all universities and take degrees if they fulfil the academic conditions, both as regards matriculation and graduation.

Foreign students of medicine, engineering, architecture, etc, number thousands, and include many North Americans. Several United States universities have established branches in Italy, at Rome, Florence, Bologna and elsewhere.

In 1967 48.1 per cent of graduates from Italian universities were the children of managers and other office workers (11.2 per cent of Italian society); only 8 per cent were the children of working class parents, who are 56.8 per cent of Italian society.

The Catholic Church has two large universities mainly for lay students, and in Rome there are half a dozen ecclesiastical universities, mainly for clerical students, and about sixty colleges. The number of religious institutes of all kinds in Rome and its province amounts to about 2,000, and there are about 40,000 clerics and probably almost as many nuns. About half the clerics resident in Rome for most of the year for studies and other purposes are foreigners.

6

How they Get About

RAILWAYS

By 1865 there were 1,362 miles of railways in the peninsula. The first railway was built, in 1839, by the kingdom of Naples and, as was usual in those days, from one royal residence to another. The Papal States were also to the fore, in spite of some doubts about the ultimate origins of the invention. Their first line, built in 1854, from Rome to Frascati, was used by the aristocracy and the Pope for· travelling back and forth to their hillside villas.

The kingdom of Piedmont began building railways for political purposes, and the Austrian monarchy built them for military purposes in its Lombardo-Venetian kingdom. Without railways Italy might never have been united materially, and neither might a national economy have been created. During the second world war three-fifths of the equipment and installations was destroyed. The effort at reconstruction is one of the best success stories of post-war Italy. All lines were running again and all bridges were rebuilt by 1947. The opportunity was taken, as in so much else, not only to restore but to improve and recreate. There is now a new ten-year plan, dating from 1962, for a further redevelopment of the whole system.

There are now 10,625 miles of permanent way, and the system is articulated in three main north-south routes—the Tyrrhenian and Adriatic lines and the central Milan-Rome-

Naples-Palermo line. There are numerous cross lines, the most notable being the one from Turin to Milan, Venice and Trieste, and the one linking Naples with Bari, Brindisi and Taranto, meeting the Adriatic line at Bari. There are a number of narrow-gauge lines, mostly in mountain districts, either privately owned or managed separately from the State lines.

Most lines are electric. The carriages are well-built, smooth-running and designed with the convenience of the passengers in mind. There are two classes, and first is much more expensive than second. There are many very fast, non-stop trains, with luxury fittings and even higher fares than ordinary first class. All long-distance trains have excellent, inexpensive restaurants. Terminal stations, such as those at Rome, Naples, Florence and Venice are all that such stations should be.

Notwithstanding keen competition from road transport, passenger traffic on all railways amounts to 31,000,000 a year. Like all continental trains, Italian trains run on the left-hand track, contrary to road traffic, which is of course right-hand. The reason is that railways came from England.

At the end of 1966 the Italian State Railways *(Ferrovie della Stato*—FS) possessed about 4,300 locomotives and about 127,000 rolling stock. During the year 21 new electric locomotives were put into service, together with 2 diesel trains, 77 diesel locomotives, 16 electric shunting engines, 15 tenders, 91 new carriages, 23 baggage and mail-wagons, and 6,520 freight trucks of various kinds. In addition 1,790 trucks, 64 carriages and a new kind of locomotive, the E-444, were brought into service, for very fast services, attaining 120 miles an hour on such lines as the Turin-Naples and Milan-Naples. The older locomotives, known as the E-646, can draw 18-20 carriages full of passengers at more than 94 miles an hour.

The position of the railways has changed from its old one of near monopoly of transport to one of free competition with road and air transport. The State Railways are accepting the challenge and making improvements in their equipment, methods and services rather than merely closing down lines on all sides. However, the present total length of over 10,000 miles will be slowly and cautiously reduced to about 7,500. But this will not all be by closures; some lines will be shortened—for example the run from Florence to Rome will be reduced through straightening from 197 miles to 163. Of level crossings, 350 are to be replaced by over and under passes, and wooden sleepers are to be replaced with precompressed-concrete ones. Times of journeys will be shortened; journeys between the regional capitals have recently all been shortened by from one to one-and-a-half hours. As driving becomes more and more difficult, dangerous and expensive, even on the motorways, the State Railways can expect to win back much traffic with their splendidly-designed, fast and perfectly-run non-stop express trains. Who would take the trouble to drive from Rome to Turin when he can get there in less than seven hours on the ' Cinque Terre ' luxury express?

Plans are also afoot to integrate rail, air and sea services, particularly in connection with transport between the mainland and the islands. Provisions for carrying cars across the sea and through mountain ranges are also being extended and improved. Finally, there will be a travel ticket known as the ' Italpass ', which will give travel on all means of transport in the peninsula, by air, land and sea, for from seven to sixty days. Electronic systems are being introduced for shunting yards and track-changing, and the State Railways foresee the day when all trains in the peninsula will run by remote control, without drivers.

Goods traffic is also to be modernised and rationalised, with better door-to-door and collection services. The net recovery of 4 per cent in the passenger traffic in the last months of 1965 was consolidated in 1966. Goods traffic increased by 4 per cent in 1965, and by 2 per cent in 1966.

Passenger fares in 1967, second class, were about 1½d a mile. The State pays very big subsidies to keep fares down.

ROADS

The road system has increased to an even greater extent in the post-war period than have the railways. It now consists of more than 22,000 miles of State highways, more than 44,000 miles of provincial roads, and some 500,000 miles of local roads. Roads and road traffic are under the control of the *Azienda Nazionale Strade Statali*, ANAS, the red control stations of which are a well known feature of all main roads. Motorways *(autostrade)* were first built in Italy (the first stretch, from Milan to Brescia, still in service, dates from 1929) and Italy still leads in this branch of engineering. Both the ANAS and the IRI, through its subsidiary *Autostrade*, build them. There are now 1,300 miles in operation, most of which were laid down in recent years. The best known is the *Autostrada del Sole*, the Highway of the Sun, which runs for 470 miles from Milan to Naples, by way of Bologna, Florence and Rome, and is now being extended from Salerno to Reggio Calabria. It has cut the motoring time from Milan to Naples by half.

A further 1,061 miles of motorways are being built, and plans are being drawn up for 608 more. This will bring the total length up to 2,969 miles (396 built by ANAS, the rest by IRI). In the year 1966, 241 miles of new motorway were brought into service. This may be compared with figures for 1966 in other countries: Great Britain 57, West Germany 89, France 72. As a photograph in this book shows, the Italian motorways are marvels of style as well as engineering, sweeping in harmonious lines, without regard for cost, through the beautiful hilly countryside. It is clear that they will rapidly become as integral a part of the landscape as are the hilltop towns and churches. In 1966 the number of vehicles using them increased by about 10 per cent over 1965.

Most of them are toll roads. They now connect all the chief cities and many of the chief regional cities, and are beginning to be extended between the provincial cities. The most spectacular project is for the great Munich-Venice highway, which will cross the Brenner Pass and descend into the valley of the Etsch-Adige. There are to be new tunnels through the Alps under Mont Blanc, and at Fréjus, Spluga and Stelvio.

The ancient Roman Consular Roads are still very much in use; the modern motorist travels over the Appian Way from

Rome to Brindisi, the Flaminian Way from Rome to Rimini, the Cassian Way into Tuscany, the Valerian Way across the Abruzzi, the Salarian Way from Rome to the Adriatic, and the Aurelian Way from Rome to Paris. There are many others. The motorway engineers have generally not been able to find better routes than those discovered by the ancient engineers.

Numbers of cars in use and motoring generally have already been discussed. Since June 1967 the Italian Automobile Club and the Fiat Company have been conducting a joint, country-wide rescue and ambulance service on all State roads during the summer. The Road Police already have such a service, *Soccorso Stradale*, but the new service will go out looking for trouble. Italians (unless they own a Fiat car) will have to pay for the help they receive, but foreigners will be helped free of charge.

The vast majority of cars on Italian roads, now approaching 7,000,000, seem to be used for pleasure driving. The old cities, which were not built with the motor car in view, are suffering greatly from this superfluity of cars, and in Rome, to mention the most notorious example, very little by way of solution to the problem has been found. The people who now drive into the centre of the city and leave their cars parked there all day, used to come by bus only five years ago. There seems to be no good reason why they should not continue to do so. There are proposals to exclude unlicensed motor traffic from the area within the city walls, except for those who live in that area, and to forbid parking until ten in the morning, thus forcing most workers to revert to buses. Commuting is not an Italian habit in the sense of the British and American custom of living even 50 and 60 miles from one's place of work. But cities are increasing in area and more and more people are living on the outskirts or in nearby villages. A recent trial scheme of establishing parking lots on the outskirts and providing a rapid shuttle-service of buses into Rome failed. Parking meters are not favoured.

Other reforms contemplated are pedestrian zones in the old city, especially around the most beautiful squares and streets.

As regards driving faults, a police report recently showed that most fines were imposed for not giving way (three times as common as all other offences); then came driving on the wrong side, illegal passing, breaking speed limits, using blinding headlights, and driving without glasses. Drunken driving is very rare indeed (only 333 cases in 1966 in the whole country), as is drunkenness in general in Italy. Motor insurance will become obligatory in 1967. Road tax is to be abolished.

The Italian drives as fast as he can, and depends for safety on the speed of his reactions and his brakes. Accidents are very common, are increasing, especially on the motorways, and are always spectacular and total. The most common form is a head-on collision at high speed, in which a dozen people, usually members of one or two families, are burnt to death—' carbonised ', as the newspapers say.

AIR TRAFFIC

Inland and international air traffic has been increasing constantly. The sole Italian airline is Alitalia, which has five subsidiaries (one in Somalia), and in which the IRI owns 96.8 per cent of the shares. It began operations in 1947 with a flight of a

———

Contemporary Rome : football and sports stadiums by the banks of the Tiber, and near the Milvian Bridge. On the left the Foro Italico; on the right the Olympic Stadium. The Olympic swimming pool is in the background.

Fiat G.12 from Turin to Rome, and has gradually absorbed all other companies. Today Alitalia uses 14 intercontinental DC-8s, with 142 seats (a new version with 189 seats has been ordered), 21 medium-range Caravelles, 16 Vickers Viscounts, used mainly on inland routes, and 3 Macchi MB 326 D two-seater training planes. It has placed orders for a further 30 medium-range Douglas DC-9s, and 4 giant Boeing B747s, with capacity for 350-450 passengers. Alitalia now flies to 53 countries and 85 cities on all five continents, and its network of 135,000 miles is the fourth biggest in the world. In 1966 it carried more than 3,263,000 passengers.

Italy is in a central position as regards air routes. A great new airport has recently been built at Fiumicino, about fifteen miles from Rome, on the coast, where the noise of air traffic is least noticeable and troublesome; there are other excellent international airports at Milan-Linate, Palermo and Venice, and many other airports for local flights. Helicopters have come into use in recent years for transport to and from airports.

WATERWAYS

Inland waterways are a very old and now an expanding

A football match with medieval rules in the Piazza della Signoria at Florence.

The 'Bridge Game', a contest, recalling a battle of 1509, is celebrated at Pisa every year on the first Sunday in June. Eight hundred men take part in it. The aim is for one side to push the other off the bridge.

I

means of transport in Italy. The system is not connected with the canals of the rest of Europe, because the Alps present an impassable barrier—obviously no longer so if it were ever considered worth while to make a waterways tunnel through them. And until now it has been impossible to reach the east coast from the west. The first and greatest Italian canal was built by Cistercian monks between 1177 and 1223; it is known as the Naviglio Grande—the Grand Navigation Canal—and runs from Abbiategrosso to Milan. It departs from the Ticino, and rejoins it south of Milan again, near Pavia, after passing through an extension known as the Bereguardo canal, finished in 1457. Leonardo da Vinci designed locks for this canal. Another one, the Naviglio di Pavia, finished in 1359, also begins from the Ticino, a little above its junction with the Po. Other old canals link Lakes Como and Maggiore, and these with the Ticino and the Adda, and the Po. There are many other irrigation and navigation canals along the middle and lower reaches of the Po, the most notable being the Mantua-Cremona canal, now being brought back into service. Plans have been laid for a waterway extending from Locarno on Lake Maggiore to Venice, by canalising streams and digging link canals. The river Po itself is navigable from its mouth on the Adriatic up to Turin, but in practice barges do not ascend further than its conjunction with the Sesia, 47 miles below Turin, near Valmacca. This disadvantage is to be remedied. Ten-tonners can go right upstream, and 100 or 120-tonners can navigate the rest in good conditions. There are also plans to make the Po navigable for 1,000-tonners as far as Mantua and Milan. Needless to say, there is an intricate system of waterways in and around Venice. There are plans to link the Po with Genoa by a canal tunnel through the Apennines, and a 7½-mile ship canal was recently opened at Ravenna. There are canals dating from several centuries along the Arno, the Tiber and in the reclaimed lands south of Rome. It is reckoned that canal transport of grain and many kinds of bulk goods costs only half or even a third as much as transport by rail or road, and is socially preferable to road transport.

STRAITS OF MESSINA

The idea of bridging the Straits of Messina is an old one. Plans are being studied for a bridge with three suspension spans with a total length of 10,000 feet, or one with six suspended spans, 11,233 feet long in all. When completed it will be one of the grandest sights in the world.

7

How they Amuse Themselves

THE THEATRE

The Italian theatre has enjoyed a revival since the war, mainly through the work of repertory companies and the system of permanent city acting companies *(teatro stabile)* subsidised from municipal funds. The best-known names are those of Giorgio Strehler, Luchino Visconti and Franco Zeffirelli, all producers, and Vittorio Gassman and Giorgio Albertazzi, actors. Such theatres exist in all the cities of any importance, most notably Rome and Milan. In Rome there are about 35 theatres, which put on repertories of Italian and foreign classics and modern plays. A feature of the theatrical life of Rome is the presence of several United States companies, which present American and Italian plays. Many theatre festivals are held during the summer. Ancient Roman and Greek plays are performed in Roman theatres at Taormina and Ostia. The Festival of the Two Worlds at Spoleto attracts Italian and English-speaking actors every summer, and similar festivals are held at Venice, Florence, Parma and Perugia. There is a National Academy of Dramatic Art.

OPERA

Opera is undoubtedly the Italian theatrical art par excellence. It is no secret that the great days of opera ended with the death of Puccini in 1924, but every year there is a long season of opera, from November to June, and a rather limited repertory of mostly Italian operas are performed. There was a time when every village of any size had its opera house (now often turned into a cinema), touring companies travelled the peninsula by the hundred, and the audiences sang the choruses with the cast. The attention given to performances is still intense, highly knowledgeable and highly critical, and to get an insight into the deeper soul of Italy one must attend a grand performance in one of the great old opera houses, such as La Scala at Milan, the Rome Opera, the San Carlo at Naples, the Teatro Ducale at Parma and many more. Open-air performances are arranged every year in many places, especially in Rome at the Baths of Caracalla.

MUSIC

There are likewise many concerts of chamber music and symphonic music in all cities and many towns during the year. A feature of Roman musical life is the number of free concerts held during the year, many of them in churches.

THE CINEMA

The cinema is another branch of the theatrical arts in which Italy has made a great name since the war. In fact many of the characteristics which have been so much praised were already present in the pre-war Italian cinema, when historical spectaculars were already an Italian speciality. Anyone interested in films will know who the leading actors and producers are, and will have seen the chief films that have been made in recent years. It is also well known that Rome is one of the centres of the world cinema. The industry has been aided and organised by a State agency since before the war, when the famous Cinecittà near Rome was built. Cinemas are required to show a high proportion of Italian films every year, and foreign films are always shown in dubbed versions, except in very expensive special cinemas in big cities. These provisions, which date from before the war, seriously limit the range of foreign films which one may see. There is nothing like the variety that may be seen in London, and there are far fewer ' art cinemas ' than in Britain. In order to see good foreign productions one must belong to a film club. The Italian film industry is characterised by much mediocrity, made for mass markets, with brilliant masterpieces such as ' Divorzio alla Italiana ' standing out against that sombre background.

The number of cinema tickets sold in Italy comes second only to the number sold in the United States. Takings in 1966 were equal to those in West Germany, France and Britain combined. Programmes begin about four in the afternoon and run continuously, the last usually beginning about eleven o'clock at night.

Every film is interrupted in the middle, and is so divided into a *Primo Tempo* and a *Secondo Tempo*. There are large numbers of very cheap cinemas where one can see old films or very popular ones; many parishes have their own cheap cinemas, which show programmes designed for children and adult programmes considered unexceptionable by the ecclesiastical censors. Film distribution is on different lines from distribution in Britain. A film of any value is first of all shown in an expensive cinema where tickets cost about 15s. or £1. This is known as *Prima Visione*; after its run there it is moved to cinemas of *Seconda Visione*, which are cheaper, finally it ends its life in the more numerous cinemas of *Terza Visione*, where it may keep on reappearing for years and where prices are as low as 1s. 6d. or 2s.

Film censorship is severer than it is in England, or rather it disapproves of different things from the British film censors, and expresses its disapproval in a different way.

RADIO AND TELEVISION

Radio broadcasts began in 1924. There are three radio programmes, The National, Second and Third, equivalent to the

British Home, Light and Third Programmes. Television began in 1954. It is a State monopoly, controlled through the IRI, as is radio, but the First Channel transmits advertisements. These are restricted to about 3½ per cent of all advertising time, and are also limited to periods of about fifteen minutes three times a day, so that one knows when to turn the set off. In fact most advertisements contain a lot of wit and ingenuity, and one is not affronted by them so much as by British television advertisements. For the rest Italian television is much like television everywhere. It reaches 98 per cent of the country and the whole of the island of Malta, where it is the only television. There are radio and television programmes in German for the population of South Tyrol. At the end of 1966 11,100,000 wireless licences were in force in Italy, and 6,235,000 of these were also for television sets. Licences cost about £8. Recent enquiries have discovered that 31 per cent of the population over the age of eighteen frequent cinemas, 63 per cent watch television, and 70 per cent listen to the wireless.

NEWSPAPERS

The Italian press displays all the characteristics of variety and diversification which are the mark of the whole peninsula. Newspapers are bought and read by 53 per cent of the population. There are about 90 daily newspapers and 6,000 periodicals (about 12,000 when all kinds of professional and trade publications are counted). About 5,880,000 copies of newspapers are printed every day. There is no mass newspaper industry, and most newspapers have quite small circulations, roughly equivalent to that of *The Times*. There are a number of old and much respected newspapers, mostly provincial ones, but with national sales : *Il Resto del Carlino* (Bologna), *Roma* (Naples), *La Nazione* (Florence). Perhaps the best known of all is the Milanese *Il Corriere della Sera*, a morning newspaper, in spite of its name ' The Evening Post '. The leading newspapers in Rome are *Il Messagero* and *Il Tempo*, and *L'Osservatore Romano*. This last, published in the afternoon by the Vatican, is required reading for anybody who wants to know what is going on in Italy—and the world, for that matter. It used to be, and to a degree still is, written in a tortuous, complicated sibylline, old-fashioned style, full of hesitations, withdrawals in mid-sentence, and endless parentheses and qualifications, but with an excellent sense of the Italian language. Its front page is as likely on any day to be printed in French or Portuguese or Latin as Italian, since it gives the full texts of papal pronouncements in their original language. The oldest newspaper in Italy is *La Gazzetta di Mantova*, founded in 1669. The *Gazzetta di Parma* is 232 years old, and at least ten others are more than a century old. The chief party political newspapers are *Il Popolo*, Christian Democrats; *Avanti!*, the Socialist Party; *Unità*, the Communist Party; *Il Secolo*, the neofascist party; *Roma* (Naples) the monarchist movement; and *La Voce Repubblicana*. A German newspaper, *Dolomiten* and periodicals are published in South Tyrol; the newspaper *Primorski Dnevnik* of Trieste is for the Slavs of Friuli-Venezia Giulia, and an American newspaper, *The Rome Daily American*, is published in Rome. The leading newspapers have very high circulations outside Italy: the *Corriere*, half its copies; *Il Tempo*, a fifth, etc.

There are a number which specialise in sensationalism, and one or two, owned by oil companies, which are edited along the lines of Anglo-Saxon popular journalism. Most Italian newspapers must be compared with *The Guardian*, *The Times* and *The Scotsman* in Britain, that is to say that they assume, and are justified in assuming, a high level of intelligence in their readers. Most of them support general liberal, *bien-pensant* policies. A feature of all Italian newspapers, even the most popular ones, is the Third Page—*la terza pagina*—devoted to literary and cultural matters. Most of the leading Italian writers in the last eighty years have contributed to one or more of these pages. The Italian style of telling the news is a faithful reflection of the Italian style of conversation. Some great event has happened; the correspondent from Moscow or Delhi begins with some general philosophical reflections about the nature of life, the civilisation of Russia, or India, as it may be, some considerations upon the character of the leading personages, and what he said to one of his colleagues last night. Very gradually the writer decides to come to the point; two or three columns on he says *ed eccoci i fatti*—' here we are at what happened '. Car accidents and thefts are recounted in the same way. The Italian journalist still writes as to an audience whose character he knows, not as to a mass, mindless and characterless.

The Catholic hierarchy owns a chain of daily papers. Weekly pictorial magazines and magazines for women flourish, as do political weeklies. There are a great many intellectual reviews.

The Italian press enjoys more freedom than the British. The British press suffers, if from nothing else, from entanglement by obstructive libel laws and government censorship. The number of things that British newspapers will not print through fear, or alleged fear, of libel actions, is infinite. Not so in Italy; comment is free, particularly before, during the course of, and after trials and court cases. It is not considered that press comments or revelations will prejudice the outcome of a trial. A headline such as ' A Wrong Decision !' is not uncommon immediately after a judge and jury have delivered a verdict. Nor do people go to law hoping for fabulous sums from libel actions. The law requires periodicals to print corrections or apologies if necessary, and that is that.

Magazines which are denounced as offending public morals and are proved to do so are sequestrated. But sequestration is only local or regional.

LIBRARIES AND PUBLISHING

There are very many ancient libraries all over Italy, in monasteries and convents and State institutions. These are all freely open to students, as are the libraries of academies, schools, colleges and universities. The National Library, which has branches in several cities, differs from the British Museum in that it is willing to lend its books. A vast new building is being erected for it in Rome. Copyright affairs are controlled by a branch of the Prime Minister's office which keeps a General Register of Protected Works. There are also a State Record Library

I*

and a Film Library. There are local municipal and other lending libraries, but nothing like the system which has been created in Britain. Instead there are many more bookshops per 1,000 of the population than there are in Britain, though Italians are less devoted than the British to reading as a way of passing the time.

SPORT AND RECREATION

All the sports played in Britain are also played in Italy, with the exception of cricket (and even that is played, among British clerical students and the British residents; a team comes from England every summer to play in Rome). Italians as a rule are not given to physical exertions of a general kind as a means of pleasure; the young men, or most of them, do not go and climb mountains, but stand in the piazza, converse and hope to speak to a girl. Golf is played by the upper and some of the middle classes; the upper classes hunt and shoot. About 50,000 Romans go out into the countryside every autumn to shoot anything edible.

Most Italians who are interested in sport—and there are many sporting newspapers and pages of sporting news in the ordinary press—watch, or partake only vicariously. Football and speed cycling are the most favoured mass sports, and every Sunday the great football stadiums in Milan, Turin, Naples, Rome, Bologna and most other cities are filled with thousands of fans, just as in England. Football has much the same characteristics in Italy as in England, and the teams are becoming more and more international in their composition.

A *Gran Giro d'Italia*—Grand Tour of Italy—occurs for cyclists every year. It is more than 1,800 miles long, and is followed on television and radio every inch of the way. When a big football match is being shown on television, streets and squares and restaurants are deserted.

The basic Italian pastime is bowls—*boccie*—played on a sanded rink, mainly in villages. Cards are popular, but gambling is forbidden except in certain casinos. Italians also like to go to the seaside and to the hills and to drive. The word for summer holidays is *villegiatura*—' going to the villa ', and it obviously descends from the time when the noble or bourgeois city dweller retired to his hill villa to escape the heat of summer. The old ritual is still observed. In July any woman who can afford it takes a seaside villa or cottage and goes there with the children. The husband remains in the city and goes down at weekends. Then in August the family goes to the mountains or hills and the husband joins them there. The cities are nowadays left to foreigners. Most city dwellers return to their native village or visit their country cousins at this time also. The beaches of Italy, regrettably, are largely in the hands of entrepreneurs, who lease long stretches, put barbed wire about them and hire them out at inflated prices. A certain kind of Italian likes to go to these places, but the Government has adopted a policy of freeing the coastline and already much has been done in this direction. And yet it is impossible for the Latin mind to leave nature completely alone, so free beaches are provided with gates which open and shut at stated times, and with *custodi*. And this brings us to the question of the Italian attitude towards sport and recreation in general.

Although sport is a spontaneous and natural expression of human behaviour, it still requires some form of organisational structure. In Italy the task of co-ordinating and supervising all sporting activities is the responsibility of the National Olympic Committee (CONI). The law instituting the Committee was approved in 1943 . . . CONI performs its task through 32 national sports federations—enjoying wide discretional powers—and over 20,000 sports clubs.

The Committee publishes a ' Review of the Law of Sport ', from which the above is taken, and there is an Institute for Credit for Sporting Installations and a Central School of Sport near Rome. Between the years 1896 and 1964 2,200 Italian athletes took part in 18 Olympic Games and won 101 gold medals, 84 silver and 79 bronze in all branches of modern sport. Italian horsemen have excelled in the Horse Trials which are held at Rome every spring. Horse-racing is not the national institution that it is in Britain, but races are held at Milan, Rome and Naples, and have a large following. There are a few city betting shops and a State betting totalisator system.

DOPOLAVORO

A feature of Italian life is the institution known as *Dopolavoro*, introduced by fascism. It provides after-work recreational and study facilities for the workers in each industry, and has taken on a wide range of related activities. The various *Dopolavoro* associations have their own beach colonies for adults and children, and so have all kinds of business and industrial organisations, ministries, and the armed services.

When spring comes, according to Chaucer, ' sollten men to go on pilgrimages '. In the summer vast numbers of people go on pilgrimages to one or other of the numerous and celebrated shrines situated all over Italy. Many, such as Loreto and Assisi, are well-known to the world, but many others have mainly local fame. Such pilgrimages are often extended to other countries, and in recent years have reached out as far as Siam and central Africa, where the faithful go to visit Catholic missions. As a rule, Italians do not feel the compulsion to leave their country for the sake of pleasure or finding a more beautiful place. The motor car is changing this attitude, however, just as other modern inventions are changing other attitudes. Considerable numbers of young Italian males visit Nordic countries in the summer.

HOLIDAYS

A fortnight's holiday with pay is the rule. Factories usually close down to give all workers leave at the same time. Holiday pay is by means of payment of a ' thirteenth ', sometimes a ' fourteenth month ', i.e. an extra month's or two months' pay.

The six-day week is the general rule in most branches of work and education, except in banking and similar activities. But the five-day week is on the way. There are about 80 national, religious and civic holidays a year, and numerous local holidays and half-holidays. August is the great holiday month, and on the Feast of the Assumption of the Virgin, 15 August, known as Ferragosto, working life comes to a standstill in the way things stop in England at Christmas. The Italian winter festivity is Epiphany or Twelfth Night, 6 January, when an old woman, the Befana, brings gifts to the children. Christmas is celebrated for what it is, though commercial interests are hard at work trying to sell the Oxford Street Christmas to Italy. Carnival is celebrated, but it has declined almost out of sight. Many festivities go on for a novena, the nine days leading up to or away from them. The workers stop work on May Day, when no buses run. School holidays are roughly the same as in England. Children are at school for about 220 days a year.

8

Hints for Visitors

ITALY is not solely a vast art gallery, nor is it a sunnier Butlin's camp, nor again is it the mere economic arrangement described in this book. Travellers should go deep into the hills and ponder the meaning of a thousand villages, soaked in age and beauty, and a people who still live in an ocean of life of which the springs are unimaginably deep, rich and healthy. One should linger in a beautiful city square by a medieval or Renascence fountain, and watch the families who spend their mornings and evenings there.

There are four main kinds of train:

> *Diretto* : non-stop, or through train.
> *Rapido* : fast train.
> *Accellerato* : *slow* train!
> *Rapidissimo* : express train.

To change trains at the next stop is *cambiare alla prossima.*

Italy is the only West European country that still gives petrol coupons. If you are not using coupons, it is better to order petrol by the price, rather than by quantity. That is to say, it is better to ask for 2,000 lire worth. ' Fill her up, please !' is *Fare il pieno, per favore!*

Groceries and vegetables are sold by the *etto*—about 4¼ oz. Tea is made with warm water everywhere. Good English tea can be bought in many shops, but it is expensive. It is wise to take the siesta in the summer, because otherwise you may not be able to stay up into the small hours, as many people in the cities do, strolling in the squares and gardens and sitting at the cafés. Museums and galleries close at half-past one, but they open at about eight in the morning. Some will open at about four or five in the afternoon in the summer. They are shut on Mondays. It is wise to drink mineral water in the summer, as everyone else does. It restores the salts lost with sweat. Ordinary water is excellent and perfectly safe. However, some taps or fountains will have a sign : *Non potabile* : not drinkable (usually because of a too high mineral content). It is customary to leave a small tip for the barman in a bar and a larger tip for the waiter who serves your meal or your coffee at a table. Italians are fond of foreigners, whom they usually admire greatly. They are a very uncritical people. The interest, courtesy and attention which the vast majority will show are not dictated in the first place by commercial calculations and hopes of profit, but by what every Italian knows as *cuore*—heart.

There are a few ways in which Italian manners differ noticeably from English manners. First of all, a man will have no inhibitions about offering his hand to a lady, and she should shake hands with him; to refuse to do so, without very good reason, is very bad manners. Only the aristocracy kiss hands. Other men may kiss women's hands on particular occasions, to show special feeling. It is not necessarily bad manners on an Italian's part if he does not stand up at the approach of a lady whom he knows. Nor does Italian etiquette require him to walk on the gutter side of the pavement. In order to avoid walking into one in the street, an Italian moves to the *right*, whereas an English person instinctively moves to the *left*. Therefore it is better to move to the right too, when in Italy. Italians of both sexes walk arm-in-arm and embrace much more freely than do English people.

It is customary when entering a bar or shop to utter the greeting ' Buon giorno ' or ' Buona sera '. Italians do this automatically, and do not wait for an answer. The answer is the same greeting. One repeats the greeting on leaving. One also greets fellow travellers, fellow hotel guests etc. in the same way at all times. At mealtimes one says ' Buon appetito !' the response to which is ' Altrettanto !'—' And the same to you !' The word for ' Look out !' is ' *attenzione!'*.

One shakes hands at every meeting with acquaintances, even several times a day. The only people whose hands one does not shake with great frequency are one's friends and very close acquaintances.

Public telephones, which are installed very abundantly in all public buildings and bars, work on the token *(gettone)* system : one buys a token and inserts it in the slot of the telephone. Inter-urban calls are made with a number of tokens.

Post offices are less frequent in Italian than in British cities. Generally speaking they are also distant from each other and not easy to find. District post offices shut for the day at two in the afternoon, but the general post office in the centre of a city never closes and provides a variety of services and conveniences not pro-vided in British general post offices : typewriters for writing cables and telegrams, a shop selling stationery (all Italian stationery shops sell writing paper and envelopes by the sheet), cards, stamps, tobacco; there is a typewriter room, where one can hire a machine by the hour; a parcel-wrapping service, and the girl behind the counter will fill your fountain pen for you if it has run dry. Code numbers for addresses have recently been introduced.

Civil service hours are from eight to two, six days a week. Hours for the public are from nine to one. Most offices work from half-past eight or nine to one, and from half-past three or four till seven. The siesta period is shorter in the north than in the south, and longer in the summer than in winter. Shops are open until half-past seven or eight. Thursday is sometimes a half holiday. Banks are open from about half-past three to five in the afternoon. They are closed all day on Saturday.

All bars and restaurants will give water to drink and allow anyone to use their lavatories. There is no need to buy anything for this.

Index

Abruzzi, 15, 43
Academies, 135
Administration, 47
Adriatic Sea, 14
Agrarian reform, 110
Agricultural produce, 112ff
Agriculture, 106
Aircraft, 95
Air Force, 59
Air traffic, 142
Alitalia, 142
Alps, 14, 15
Ancona, 42
Aosta, Val d', 40
Apennines, 14, 15
Apulia, 43
Aquila, 43
Area, of Italy, 14
Army, 51
Artificial fibres, 101
Artisans and craftsmen, 102
Aspromonte, 15

Banking and banks, 103, 160
Bari, 43
Bars, 117, 159
Basilicata, 43
Birthrate, 23
Bologna, 42
Bridges, 147
Bureaucracy, 45-6

Calabria, 43
Campania, 23
Campobasso, 43
Carabinieri, 64
Casa per il Mezzogiorno, 116
Catholic Church, 49, 81, 83
Celts, 21
Cheese, 77
Chemical Industry, 98
Cinema, 149
Cities, 23, 40-4
Civil Service, 45-6, 160
Climate, 19
Communes, 44
Constitution, 36-40
Corno, Mt, 15
Cotton, 101
Council of State, 46-7
Court of Accounts (Corte dei Conti) 46-7
Court procedure, 62
Crafts, 102
Criminal jurisdiction, 61
Currency, 50

Death Penalty, 63, 66
Death Rate, 23
Dialects, 24
Dolomites, 14
Dopolavoro, 156
Drinks, 75, 159

Driving, 142
Drunkenness, 142

Education, 130
Electricity, 85
Electronics, 98
Emilia, Romagna, 42
Employers' Organisations, 123
Engineering industries, 93,
    96, 97
*Ente Nazionale Energia Elet-
    trica*, 46
Ente Nazionale Idrocarburi,
    ENI, 46, 86
Enti, 45-6
Etiquette, 159

Factories, 84, 156
Fanfani, Amintore, 48, 49
Fascism, 12, 34, 156
Feasts and festivities, 157
Finance, 103
Fisheries, 115
Florence, 19, 42
Food, 75
Foreign Policy, 49
Forests, 115
Friuli, Venezia Giulia, 23, 42
Fruit growing, 114

Galleries, 159
Genoa, 14, 41
Geography, 13
Germans, 21
Government, 39
Gran Paradiso, 14
Gran Sasso d'Italia, 15
Grants, educational, 135

History, 29

Holidays, 156
Hospitals, 81
Housing, 67

Industrialisation and Industry,
    84
Institutes, 135
Insurance, 129
Ionian Sea, 14
Iron and Steel, 92
*Istituto per la Ricostruzione
    Industriale*, IRI, 45, 85, 92,
    93, 95, 103-4, 142
Italy, area, 14
    Upper, 14, 15
    history, 29

John XXIII, Pope, 48

Kiev, 87

Lakes, 16
Land reclamation, 110
Language, 24
Latium, 23
Law, 39
Legal system, 59
    profession, 60
Libraries, 153
Liguria, 23, 41
Ligurian Sea, 14
Local government, 44
Lombardy, 15, 41

Malta, 13
Manners, Italian, 159
Marble, 91
Marches, 42

Marriage, 23
Mattei, Enrico, 86
Matterhorn, 14
Meals, 76
Medical Services, 80
Messina, Straits of, 147
Methane, 89
Mezzogiorno, 22, 105, 110, 116, 121
Michelangelo, 91
Milan, 14
Mineral resources, 92
Ministries, 45
Molise, 43
Monte Cervino (Matterhorn), 14
Monte Rosa, 14
Moro, Aldo, 48
Motor Insurance, 142
Motor vehicles, 94
Motorways, 140
Museums and galleries, 159
Music, 150
Mussolini, Benito, 34, 47

Naples, 43
National characteristics, 25
National Economic Council, CNEL, 47
Navy, 58
Newspapers, 151
Nuclear energy, 86

Opera, 149

Palermo, 44
Papacy, 48, 49
Passes, Alpine, 14
Penal System, 59
Pensions, 82, 129

Petroleum, 86
Piedmont, 40
Pilgrimages, 156
Pipelines, 87, 88, 91
Po, river, 14
   valley, 15, 16
Police, 64
Political parties, 47
Poor Relief, 129
Ports *see* Seaports
Post offices, 160
Potenza, 43
Press, the, 151
Publishing, 153

Racial derivations, 20
Radio, 150
Railways, 137, 158
Ravenna, 99
Recreation, 154
Reggio Calabria, 43
Regions, 40-4
Religion, 49-50
Restaurants, 76-7, 159
Revolution, French, 11
   Industrial, 11
Rimini, 14
Risorgimento, 33
Rivers, 15, 16, 19
Roads, 139
Road Tax, 142
Rome, 43, 81
Rubber, 99

San Marino, Republic of, 14
Sardinia, 13, 19
Schools, 130
Seaports, 121
Seasons, 19
Shares in Industry, 39, 105
Shipbuilding, 93

Shipping, 121
Shops and Shopping, 116, 158, 159
Shopping hours, 117, 160
Sicily, 13, 19, 43
Sickness and injury benefits, 82, 128
Sila, 15
Slavs, 21
Social Security, 82, 128
South *see Mezzogiorno*
Spending habits, 78, 118
Sport, 154
States, historical, 29-34, 44
Steel, 92
Stock exchange, 105

Taxation, 50
Television, 151
Textiles, 100
Theatre, 148
Trade, domestic, 116
foreign, 119
Trades Unions, 122
Traffic problems, 141
Trent, 41
Trentino, 41
Trieste, 42, 87, 122
Turin, 40
Tuscany, 23, 42

Tyrol, South, 41
Tyrrhenian Sea, 14

Umbria, 42
Unemployment, 127
Universities, 133

Vatican City, 14
Vegetables, 113
Veneto, 41
Venezia Giulia *see* Friuli
Venice, 41
Ventimiglia, 13
Verona, 41
Villeggiatura, 155
Vines, 113
Virgil, 11
Volcanoes, 15

Water, 159
Waterways, 145
Winds, 20
Wine, 77-8
Women at work, 127
Wool, 101
Work, 84
Working hours, 160